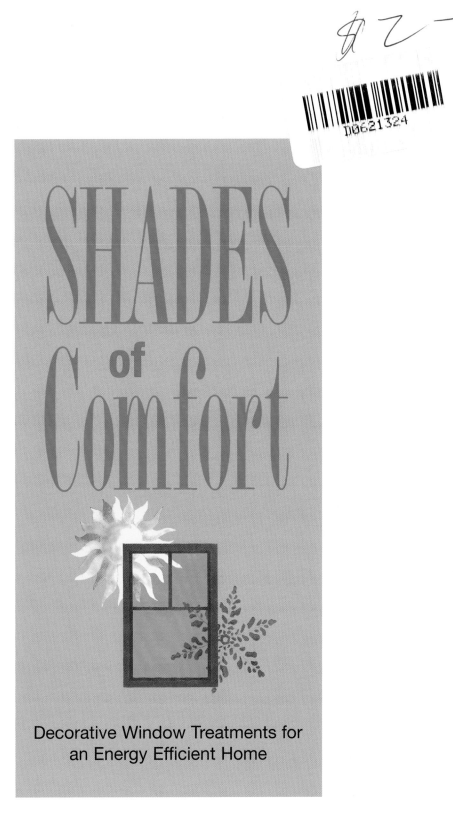

SHADES of Comfort

Decorative Window Treatments for an Energy Efficient Home

Complete Directions for Making Flat Roman, Balloon, Hobbled, and Side-draw Styles Using Warm Window®

Writer & Editor

Jill Owen

Technical Editor

Barbara Weiland

Graphic Designer

Jeannie Davison

Cover Design and Illustrations

Jil Johänson

Typographer

Rosemary Widener

Production

Tavo Adame

Keith Thygerson

Leanne Penfield

Photographer

Mike Zens

*Window Treatments
designed and sewn by*

Barbara Munson

Window on Page 12 courtesy of
Weathervane Window Co.,
Woodinville, WA

Shades of Comfort
©1996 The Warm Company

The Warm Company
16110 Woodinville-Redmond Rd., #4
Woodinville, WA 98072
1-800-234-WARM

Printed in the Unites States of America
ISBN# 0-9654466-0-3

The information in this book is presented in good faith, but no warranty is given nor
results guaranteed. Since The Warm Company has no control over the user's choice
of materials or procedures, the Company assumes no responsibility for the use
of this information.

Many thanks to Louise Brown, The Sewing Company, Wenatchee, WA, for her creative
use of Warm Window in developing the Hobbled and Balloon shade patterns.

TABLE OF CONTENTS

WHY A WARM WINDOW®?

In the past, almost everyone would have agreed that price, appearance, durability, and easy maintenance were the universally important considerations when purchasing window treatments for a home. Today, however, energy efficiency tops that list for many homeowners due to increasing national and global emphasis on the environment, and preserving and conserving the world's resources for generations to come.

This is probably why you're considering Warm Window for your current window covering project.

Your windows are usually responsible for the greatest amount of heat loss in your home – even if you have storm windows or the newer dual pane thermal windows. As a result, the window covering you choose can have a tremendous impact on energy consumption. Many treatments available today have some insulating capacity, but consider this: the R-value of a single thick window is increased from 1.3 to an astonishing 7.69 with Warm Window shades installed. Warm Window works as well to keep rooms cool in the summer as it does to reduce heat loss in the colder months. Regulating heat loss or gain means extra savings on expensive energy bills which is why your investment in Warm Window will pay for itself many times over.

Warm Window is a unique window treatment concept that actually increases the R-value (page 2) of your windows and makes your home more comfortable in any climate, at any time of the year. The bonus? You save on expensive heating and cooling costs while saving energy – beautifully. Consider the additional benefits:

Warm Window shades –
- Add comfort and style to your home.
- Reduce window heat loss by more than 81%.
- Inhibit solar heat gain by up to 79%.
- Reduce heating and cooling costs.
- Make rooms dark for daytime sleeping.
- Reduce noise pollution from outside sources.
- Add resale value to your home.
- Help save Mother Earth's natural resources.

In a nutshell, reducing heat loss or gain by using Warm Window shades in your home saves money, conserves fossil fuel, and makes your home more comfortable. When you consider the myriad benefits of covering your windows with Warm Window shades, you're sure to agree they're the sensible and "cent-sible" solution to dressing your windows in style for personal comfort and energy efficiency.

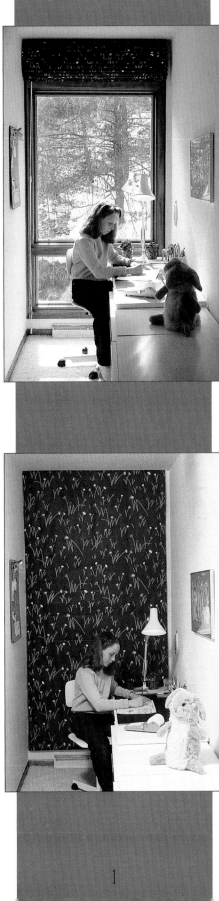

1

WARM WINDOW® BASICS

"My daughter's bedroom and mine are on the north side of our house. We were never warm in the winter months until we had our Warm Windows installed."
Pam Lapp, Fort Collins, CO

You don't have to be an expert at sewing to make Warm Window shades. Even beginners have success following our step-by-step instructions for measuring windows and making and installing beautiful shades. The directions in this book have been expanded to include decorative shade styles in addition to the basic Flat Roman shade for which Warm Window was originally designed. You'll find special chapters on each of the options – Balloon, Hobbled, and Side-draw shades.

For those who would rather not sew, we have also included dozens of time-saving "No Sew" tips using Steam-A-Seam 2®, the fabric fusing web that joins fabrics permanently with the touch of an iron.

Before you begin your Warm Window project, it will be helpful to understand some basic information about energy efficient window treatments and how the patented Warm Window fabric works to keep you warmer in cold climates and cooler in hot ones.

WHAT'S ALL THIS TALK ABOUT R-VALUE?

The effectiveness of any material in preventing energy from flowing though it is defined in terms of R-value. The higher the R-value of a given material, the greater its insulating capacity. The following chart gives approximate R-values for various materials.

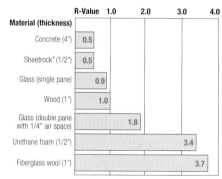

The effectiveness of Warm Window shades was tested independently by Architectural Testing, Inc. of York, PA. The results showed that the R-value of a wood-frame, single-glazed window went from 1.39 to an impressive 7.69 with the addition of a Warm Window shade.

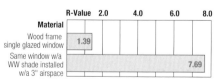

The same test results further proved that Warm Window inhibits heat loss by more than 81%. It also reflects away up to 79% of unwanted solar heat radiation. As with any product, the best test is the one you conduct yourself. Testimonials from homeowners who have chosen Warm Window for their window coverings are the best evidence of how well this product works.

HOW THE WARM WINDOW SYSTEM WORKS

- During a cold spell, do certain rooms or parts of rooms still feel cold even after you've turned the thermostat up?
- Does the sun wake you up on mornings when the alarm doesn't?
- Is the sun overheating your home and causing unsightly fading of expensive furniture and carpeting?
- Do you stay clear of the sliding glass doors in your kitchen or family room to avoid drafts?

If you answered "yes" to any of these questions, you are experiencing some simple fundamentals of physics: *Conduction, Convection, Infiltration, and Radiation.* These are the four ways heat is lost through windows. Warm Window works to combat all four types of heat loss with its patented four-layer construction. Here's how:

Conduction

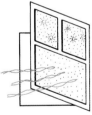

Heat energy travels by conduction through any material (air included) moving from warm to cold. The patented Warm Window system is designed to reduce heating energy loss from conduction. Dead-air space around the layers of the needle-punched Dacron Holofil® and other polyester fibers used in its construction slow the conductive heat movement.

Infiltration

Warm air leaking to the cold outside through cracks around windows, doors, and other openings is called infiltration. The Warm Window polyethylene vapor and infiltration barrier work together with the magnetic edge seal to substantially reduce window heat loss from infiltration.

Convection

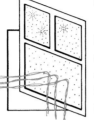

Warm air inside your home is cooled when it comes in contact with cold window glass. As it cools, it becomes more dense and is drawn downward by gravity. At the same time, replacement warm air is drawn to the cold window. The convection loop that results creates the cold draft near the floor that you often feel in a room with a window. The magnetically sealed Warm Window system prevents cooled air next to the window from escaping into the room, thereby reducing heat loss by convection.

Radiation

Heating energy is also transmitted by electromagnetic waves. This radiant energy can heat a surface that it strikes without heating the air through which it passes. Any warm object radiates a portion of its heat in this manner. For example, warmth from our bodies and solid objects in our homes radiates through windows and walls. Radiant heat can be reflected back toward its source by a reflective barrier of aluminum. Warm Window has layers of Mylar® film and polyethylene film that have been electrostatically coated with a thin layer of aluminum to reflect the radiant heat back into your home. These same radiant barriers reflect solar gain and help keep your home cool in the summer.

"Warm Window shades make a huge difference in the house during the summers. They make my rooms 10-15 degrees cooler in the summer. There is a noticeable difference in temperature between the rooms that have Warm Window shades and the ones that don't."
Janice Robinson, Portland, ME

3

THE WARM WINDOW SYSTEM

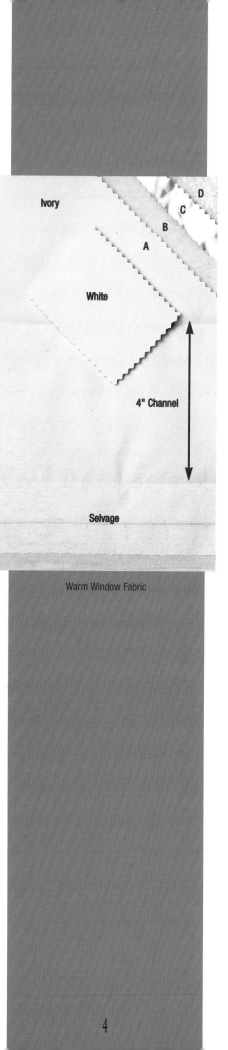

Warm Window Fabric

The Warm Window system of window covering requires three basic components: insulated fabric, magnetic tape, and your choice of decorator cover fabric.

Warm Window Fabric

Warm Window fabric consists of four layers, quilted together in 4" wide lengthwise channels designed to reduce the flow of energy through your window glass.

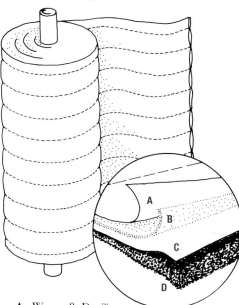

A. Warm & Dry™
   lining with fabric protector
B. High Density needled
   Dacron Holofil II®
C. Reflective polyethylene
   moisture vapor barrier
D. Metallicized Mylar with
   air-trapping fibers

Sold in widths of 48" or 56", Warm Window fabric is cut so the channels run horizontally in the completed Flat Roman, Hobbled, and Balloon style shades. (Warm Window widths are easily seamed together for shades wider or longer than the bolt width, as shown in the illustrations on page 22.) Use Warm Window with the channels running vertically for Side-draw shades. Each of these shade styles is illustrated on page 8-9.

Select Warm Window with your preference of white or ivory lining. The lining will face the outside in the completed window covering and you will cover the fuzzy Mylar side with your choice of decorator fabric.

Magnetic Tape

The shade's airtight seal is achieved by affixing Warm Window adhesive-backed magnetic tape to the window frame (or wall) and short magnetic strips to the inside edge of the shade. When the shade is completed, the magnetic strips, although covered by the decorator fabric, attach to the tape on the window frame to help seal out drafts.

Magnetic tape is available in two different forms. The continuous lengths are used for mounting on the window trim or wall. Convenient, pre-cut, 3½" long strips are used inside the shade. Polarity direction is marked on each strip. The wall mounted tape can be painted with latex or enamel to blend with the wall or trim color. Paint does not affect its ability to hold a seal.

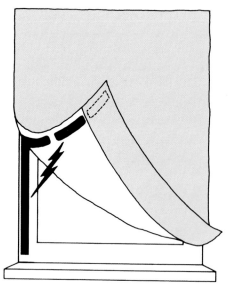

Decorator Cover Fabric

You will cover the side of your Warm Window shade that faces the room with a decorative fabric of your choice. The cover fabric should be tightly woven, of light to medium weight, and made of cotton or a cotton/polyester blend. Fabrics with fabric protector are an excellent choice for window coverings. Test the magnetic strips to see if they will attract securely through the fabric of your choice.

- Avoid highly textured or pile fabrics as they may interfere with the magnetic seal.
- Avoid loosely woven or stretch fabrics.
- Avoid fabrics with horizontal stripes as they may interfere visually with the folds in the shade.

"Warm Window satisfies both my husband and myself; he likes the savings on the heating bill, and I like shopping for all those gorgeous fabrics at the fabric stores. Sewing Warm Window is as easy as sewing a pillow case."

Jackie Trute, Ravenna, Michigan

WINDOW TYPES

Warm Window shades can be adapted for use with most any window type. To determine the right Warm Window mounting style for your window, read through the descriptions and refer to the mounting styles listed on the left.

Double-Hung Windows

Check the top of the window to see if a flat surface exists for mounting. Use a hybrid mount or an outside mount.

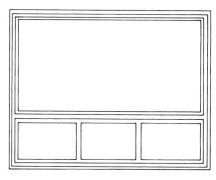

Picture Windows

These may be simple, wide expanses of glass but more often are a combination type with a fixed center sash and double-hung, casement, or awning windows at the sides. You may treat these as one unit or make shades to cover individual sections.

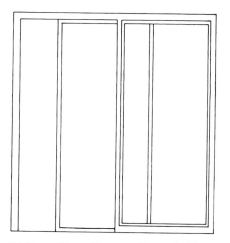

Sliding Glass Doors, French Doors

Treat the entire area as one unit. The Side-draw shade is an excellent choice, or you can mount the shade above the doors, flush with the ceiling if desired, using the Flat Roman style. Use pulleys (page 29) in place of screw eyes for ease in raising and lowering the shade.

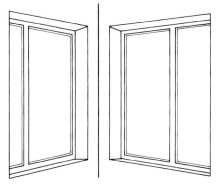

Corner Windows

Choose the mounting method according to the window type. If the frame between the windows is narrow, address the possibility of shades interfering with each other by using an inside mount or hybrid mount. You may need to open the shades one at a time and adjust the folds at the top of each one.

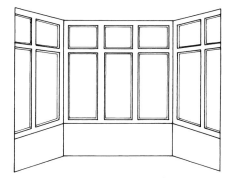

Bay and Bow Windows

Make a separate shade for each window and use either a hybrid or an inside mount. Be sure to match the fabric pattern from window to window as you would when making any other type of window treatment. Avoid an outside mount as the shades will not raise properly.

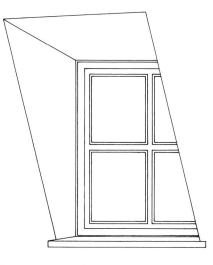

Dormer Windows

Usually deeply recessed, this window type requires a hybrid or an inside mount.

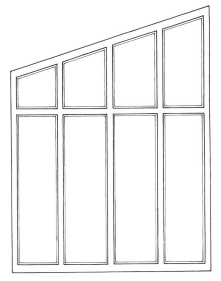

Cathedral Window

The shade top must be cut to conform to the window slant. Make a paper pattern of the window shape for precise fit and select the mounting based on the actual window type.

Skylight, Studio and Dome Windows

These windows may be fitted with special installations mounted on the slant or horizontally.

For directions using the Warm Window track for skylights call Customer Service at 1-800-234-WARM.

For additional information about measuring and trim details, see pages 12–13.

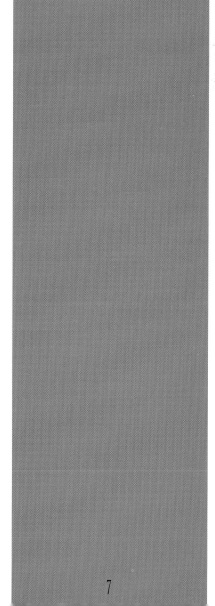

SHADE STYLES

Decorative Variations

By combining fabrics, adding borders and trim, or using appliqué to embellish your shades, you can create a custom look for your home with any of the Warm Window shade types. The use of a top treatment such as a valance is another great way to add style and distinction to your Warm Window project.

"By using decorative top treatments, Warm Window works great in the living room, dining room and family room. Balloon and Hobbled Warm Windows also add a nice touch to any room."
JoAnn Bekjern, Missoula, MT

Before you begin your Warm Window project, choose from the shade options shown here, selecting the one that best suits your style, the window, and the home setting where it will be used.

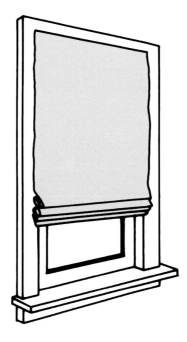

Flat Roman Shade

Flat Roman shades have a crisp, tailored appearance that complements any decor. This type of shade is raised and lowered by a system of cords and rings on the back. It is flat when lowered and forms pleats when raised. This is the most economical of all shade styles to make.

Hobbled Shade

Unlike the Flat Roman shade, the Hobbled shade maintains its soft folds, even when the shade is lowered. In order to achieve this look, the outer fabric is first attached to a lining that wraps around the Warm Window fabric. This allows the Warm Window fabric to hang flat when lowered. You will need to purchase approximately twice as much cover fabric for this shade type as you would for the Flat Roman shade.

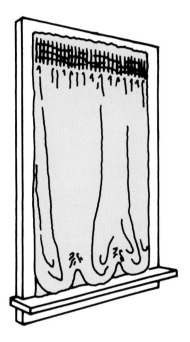

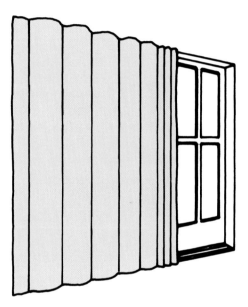

Balloon Shade

The lush fullness of this style lends a softer look to your window. Shirring tape is used to gather the outer fabric, which is then sewn to the Warm Window backing. This style requires about twice as much cover fabric as the Flat Roman shade.

Side-draw Shade

The Side-draw shade is perfectly suited to French doors, sliding glass doors, or large windows with little overhead stacking space. The quilted channels run vertically in the finished shade instead of horizontally as they do in the other styles. A special track system, available as a kit, is all you'll need to install your Side-draw shade.

TOOLS AND EQUIPMENT

Workroom Tips

Because your Warm Window® project is likely to take a day or more to complete, find a place to spread out your equipment where it will be undisturbed. This will save time and make your job much easier. If you don't have a large work table, try covering a sheet of plywood with an old sheet and setting it on some saw horses for a temporary work surface. This can also double as an ironing board if you pad it with quilt batting or an old blanket under the sheet.

• Set up a card table next to your sewing machine to hold the weight of your shade. Without this extra space for support, the weight of the shade will pull away from the needle causing crooked seaming and broken sewing machine needles.

• Make sure you have adequate lighting.

• Assemble all of your equipment before you begin. If you don't own everything on the list, consider working with a partner and dividing your purchases to keep the expenses down.

• If you are making more than one shade, make one first from start to finish to become familiar with all of the steps before you begin the rest of your shades.

• Keep your shade measurements handy. Also jot down the cut size and finished size of your Warm Window fabric and cover fabric.

• The less you move your project, the more accurate your results. Try to complete as many steps as possible on your work table.

The following items are necessary to make your shade project a success.

The Basics

• **Sewing Machine** – Make sure it is in good working order, oil it if needed, and put in a new size 16/100 or 14/90 universal needle before you begin. (Ball point needles are not recommended.)

• **Household Iron and Press Cloth** – You can use a standard press cloth or substitute any cotton or cotton blend fabric scrap.

• **Scissors or Rotary Cutter, Ruler and Mat** – Make sure the blade(s) is sharp.

• **Staple Gun** – An electric model is helpful but not necessary.

• **Screwdriver or Drill with Screw-driving Bit**

• **Steel Ruler** – This doubles as a straight edge.

• **Steel Measuring Tape.**

• **Carpenter's Square or T-Square.**

• **Needle and Thread.**

• **Hacksaw.**

• **Large, Flat Work Surface.**

• **Clear Nail Polish or White Glue.**

Optional Materials

Repositionable **Spray Adhesive** – This is recommended for adhering your cover fabric to the Warm Window fabric when making Side-draw shades (page 62) or when rings are applied through the Warm Window fabric only (page 28).

Hook and Loop Tape – Choose the sew-on type (not glue-on or self-stick) in the 1" or 2" width for attaching the shade to the mounting board.

Steam-A-Seam 2® – This fusible web has a special adhesive on both sides that eliminates steps in assembling Warm Window shades. Refer to the general directions on page 11 for using this product.

T-Shooter System – Use a T-Shooter to apply rings to your Warm Window shade without sewing. This significantly reduces shade-making time. Simply insert the needle into the shade and squeeze the trigger to attach the rings to the shade in the same way that price tags are attached to clothing.

Quicker Quilter – Similar to the T-Shooter, this tool is used to tack the shade front to the Warm Window fabric when making Side-draw shades. A nearly invisible plastic "T" is deposited on both front and back of shade, holding shade layers together. See page 74.

(left to right, top to bottom)

Steam-A-Seam	Steam-A-Seam 2
Quicker Quilter	T-Shooter

HOW TO USE STEAM-A-SEAM 2®

**Using Steam-A-Seam 2
to Make No-Sew Seams**

1. Position Steam-A-Seam 2 with the sticky side down along the right side of one edge of fabric to be seamed and remove the paper covering.

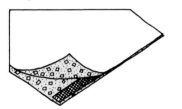

2. Align the fabrics to be bonded.

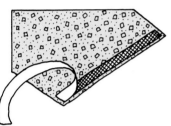

3. With your iron setting on cotton, use a damp presscloth and steam fabrics to be bonded by holding the iron in one place for ten seconds. Repeat this procedure over the entire area to be fused. Using a presscloth helps to prevent scorching and will help in the fusing process by creating additional steam.

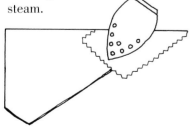

4. Unfold layers of fabric and press seam open.

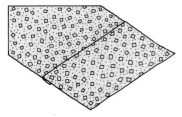

**Using Steam-A-Seam 2
to Make No-Sew Hems**

1. Position Steam-A-Seam 2 with the sticky side down on the wrong side of fabric to be hemmed and remove the paper covering.

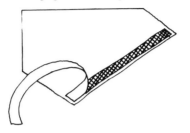

2. Fold edge of fabric over and fuse as in step 3 for seams.

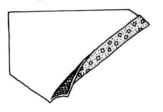

3. Press hem up desired width and place strip of Steam-A-Seam 2 under previously fused edge.

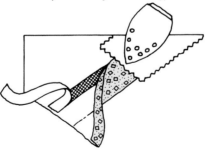

4. Fuse

Steam-A-Seam 2 is an adhesive-backed fusing web for fabric that makes it possible to complete seams and hems without sewing. The ½" size is a perfect time saver for making all types of Warm Window shades. Look for helpful No-Sew Tips throughout this book if you prefer this method of construction.

Steam-A-Seam 2 has adhesive on both sides making it easy to reposition for hems and seams. Steam-A-Seam is also available with one adhesive surface and is just as easy to use.

Use an ironing board or pad a work surface with a few layers of woolen blanket and cover it with a cotton cloth or sheet. This will help the steam from your iron to penetrate the fibers in your fabric thoroughly and fuse the Steam-A-Seam 2 most effectively. Prior to working on your finished shade, it is a good idea to do a test with your cover fabric to make sure it will accept Steam-A-Seam 2.

WARM WINDOW®
ROMAN SHADE BASICS

For general information about Warm Window shade construction, read through these directions before making any of the shade styles in this book.

When measuring your windows, check the measurements at both sides and at the top and bottom; these dimensions may vary on some windows. Measure the window diagonally from corner to corner making sure it is "square." Then measure again diagonally from the other two corners. If the window is square, these two measurements match.

If the window is not square, consider using an outside or a hybrid mount (page 15) rather than an inside mount. Remember that you will need at least ¾" space on each side of your window in which to attach the magnetic tape.

In this chapter you will find basic information about the components of Warm Window shades for the Flat Roman, Balloon and Hobbled shade styles. Detailed instructions are given for measuring your windows and determining your shade size. Additional helpful worksheets are included in the appendix for recording your window measurements and finished shade sizes.

MEASURING YOUR WINDOWS

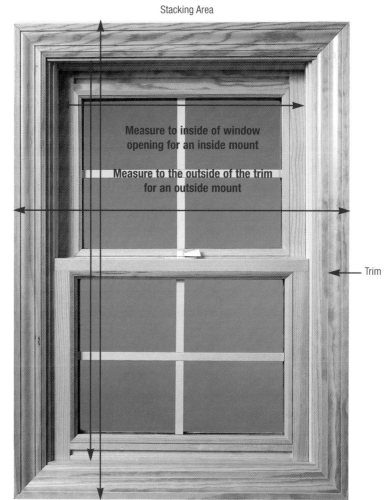

Stacking Area

Measure to inside of window opening for an inside mount

Measure to the outside of the trim for an outside mount

Trim

When measuring your windows and considering which mounting option to choose, consider the following:

• Does your window have decorative trim surrounding it, or no trim at all?
• Do you wish to conceal the trim around your window or allow it to show when the shade is lowered?
• Is there a spot on your trim that will accept the magnetic tape?

• How much space is there above the window for stacking?
• Are there any light switches or heat vents that could interfere with the shade operation?
• If there are multiple windows in a room, how can the shades be mounted to create a consistent appearance from window to window?

WHAT ABOUT WINDOW SILLS?

If your window has a sill, measure to the sill for the finished length of the shade. It will rest on the sill when it is closed.

If your window has no trim, the shade should extend past the window opening at least 2" to ensure a good seal at the bottom.

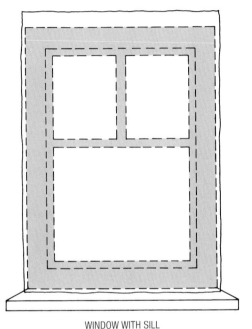

WINDOW WITH SILL

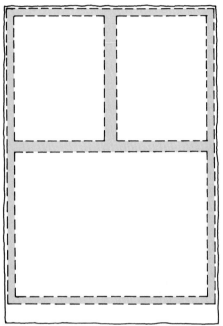

SHADE OVER WINDOW WITHOUT TRIM

"When it's 30 degrees below zero here in Montana, I can sit right next to the window and not freeze. Warm Window is worth its weight in gold!"
Lois DeFord, Helena, MT

If your window has no sill, and there is decorative trim surrounding your window, the shade should extend past the window opening to cover the trim for the most professional look.

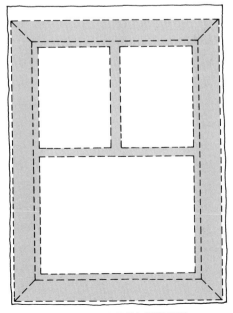

WINDOW WITHOUT SILL, WITH TRIM

DETERMINING THE FINISHED SHADE SIZE

Examine the illustrations included here to choose the best method of mounting for your window, then calculate the finished shade size for each window. Even if a group of windows appears to be the same size, be sure to measure each window carefully and do the calculations for each window size separately.

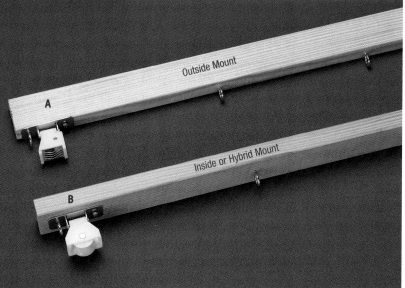

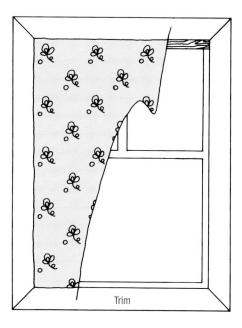

A. Mounting board is installed with the wider surface against the wall for an outside mount.

B. Mounting board installs with its wider surface against the inside of the window for inside and hybrid mounts.

Inside Mount

- Choose an inside mount when the shade is to fit completely inside the window opening.

- The window opening must be square for the shade to fit snugly.

- It may be necessary to add ¾" x ¾" moulding inside the window opening at the sides to attach the magnetic tape for a completely snug edge seal.

- The mounting board is installed inside at the top of the window frame.

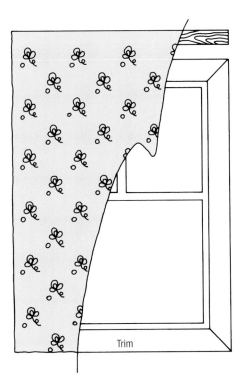

Outside Mount

- The outside mount is ideal for most windows.

- It can be used on windows with or without trim.

- With this mount, you draw the shade up completely above the window so the glass is not blocked by the fully opened shade in any way.

- The shade extends beyond the window opening a minimum of ¾" on each side. Extending the shade to the outside edge of the trim is common.

- The shade mounts to the wall above the window with the wider side of the mounting board turned flat against the wall.

Hybrid Mount

- This mount combines features of the inside and the outside mounts.

- It is suitable for windows with or without trim.

- The shade may not cover the window trim when it is closed.

- This is a good mount for windows that are not "square."

- The mounting board is installed to the inside top of the window frame.

- The shade stacking area will be within the window opening, covering some of the window glass.

- The shade extends beyond the window opening a minimum of ¾" on each side, providing a place to attach the magnetic tape.

Your shade can be attached to the mounting board using Hook & Loop tape for easy installation and repositioning.

NOTE: When deciding on the finished shade size, make an allowance for possible shrinkage caused by atmospheric moisture. Although the potential for shrinkage is very slight, cotton or cotton blend cover fabrics could shrink as much as one percent over time. This is a particularly important consideration when making very large shades. Allowing a little extra overlap at each side ensures a seal at the edge even with some shrinkage.

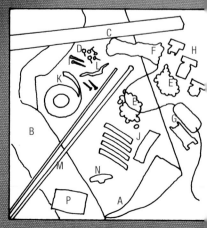

Warm Window®
INSULATED FABRIC
U.S. patent No. 4397346
CARE INSTRUCTIONS
VACUUM regularly.
For cleaning use non-immersion pressurized solvent
cleaning methods such as provided by SERVPRO
dealers.
NOTICE: Immersion in dry cleaning solvent may
damage the adhesive on the magnetic tape.
Soap and water washing may cause uneven
shrinkage.

Scotchgard

ANATOMY OF A ROMAN SHADE

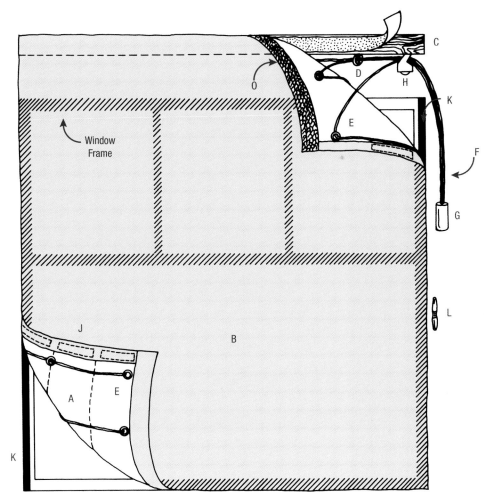

To determine the amount of Warm Window insulated fabric, magnetic tape, and other hardware required for your window measurements, please refer to the chart on the inside back cover of this book.

A. **Warm Window**

B. **Cover Fabric**

C. **Mounting Board** – The shade is attached to a 1" x 2" fabric-covered mounting board to fit the inside the window measurement for a hybrid or inside mount. For an outside mount, cut the mounting board the finished shade width.

D. **Screw Eye** – Attached to the mounting board, you will need one screw eye for each cord to guide it to the pulley.

E. **Rings** – The rings guide the cord and are placed in vertical rows at 8" to 12" intervals on every other horizontal channel quilting line. Choose from durable plastic or attractive brass rings for your shades.

F. **Cord** – Available in 1mm and 2mm diameters, the special Warm Window cord runs along the back of the shade and through the pulley to open and close the shade. The strong cord will stay flexible and will not yellow or become brittle with age.

G. **Cord Reel** – This is a combination cord pull and storage unit for the extra length of cording that hangs down when your shade is elevated. It keeps the cords safely away from small children and pets.

H. **Pulley** – The pulley is the cord guide at the operating end of the shade. Choose the standard or the locking pulley for shades up to 5 feet wide. Do not use the locking pulley on larger

shades. Standard pulleys may replace one or all screw eyes (E) on shades over several feet wide.

I. **Mounting Screws** – These 2" long screws are used to attach the mounting board to the window frame or wall. Molly screws or toggle bolts may be needed if the shade cannot be attached to wall studs.

J. **Magnetic Strips** – These pre-cut 3½" long pieces go inside the shade between quilted channels along the outer edges. They grab the magnetic tape (K) on the window trim or wall.

K. **Magnetic Tape** – This continuous length of tape is attached to the wall or the window trim to attract the magnetic strips inside the shade.

L. **Cleat** – When the shade is elevated with a standard pulley, the cord is wrapped around a cleat to hold the shade in the desired position.

M. **Weight Bar** – A ⅜" diameter round or oval, steel or aluminum weight bar is required at the bottom of the shade to give it rigid stability. The Warm Window weight bar consists of pipe sections and rods that slip inside the pipe. You can join sections of the weight bar by staggering the joints of each pipe and rod.

N. **T-Handle** (optional) – The T-Handle replaces casement window cranks that would otherwise protrude into the shade. This is necessary for the shade to fit flush to the window.

O. **Hook and Loop Tape** (optional) – Use this for easy installation and repositioning of the completed shade.

P. **Care Label** (optional)

FLAT ROMAN SHADE

Roman Shades have a crisp tailored appearance that complements any decor. This style shade is flat when lowered and forms pleats when raised. Any number of variations are possible with this versatile shade style by combining fabrics, adding borders, embellishing with appliqué, or adding a decorative top treatment such as a valance.

FLAT ROMAN SHADE

General information on preparing your cover fabric and Warm Window fabric is included in this section as well as basic shade assembly. Read through these directions before you begin your Flat Roman, Balloon or Hobbled shade.

The Warm Window fabric must be cut the exact finished width of your shade and 4" longer than the finished shade length for mounting allowance. Depending on which mounting allowance you choose, some of this extra length will be trimmed off prior to installing the shade.

The cover fabric must be cut 3½" wider and 12½" longer than the finished shade dimensions. After sewing the cover fabric to the Warm Window fabric, the extra width of the cover fabric wraps around to the back of the Warm Window fabric. The extra length provides for a 4" mounting allowance and an 8½" wide hem allowance. Use the worksheet below to calculate the cut sizes for each of your shades.

When cutting the Warm Window fabric, leave the selvage intact. It will be included in the hem.

ROMAN SHADE WORKSHEET

If you have not yet determined the finished size for your shade, return to page 14 and measure your windows as described for the type of mount you plan to use. To calculate the cut sizes for your Warm Window fabric and your cover fabric, fill in the blanks below.

Cover Fabric Cut Size

Cover Fabric Cut Width = Finished Shade Width [ ] " + 3½" = [ ] "

Cover Fabric Cut Length = Finished Shade Length [ ] " + 12½" = [ ] "

Warm Window Fabric Cut Size

Warm Window Cut Width = Finished Shade Width [ ] "

Warm Window Cut Length = Finished Shade Length [ ] " + 4" = [ ] "

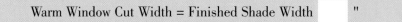

Additonal worksheets in Appendix for easy reproduction.

CUTTING THE WARM WINDOW INSULATED FABRIC

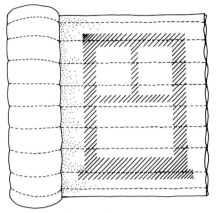

Warm Window Fabric

Warm Window is available in two widths, 48" and 56". Both sizes have two selvage edges. The width of the selvages is not included in the width, and so it can be used for the seam allowances when seaming widths together to fit your window dimensions.

When one width of Warm Window is too short for your window, you can add another width to it by stitching a horizontal seam along a line of channel quilting in the first piece. Selvage edges are then trimmed off, so that when the fabric is opened up, the channel lines remain an equal 4" apart.

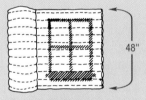

48"

One 48" width of Warm Window = Finished shade length up to 44"/ Cut shade length up to 48"

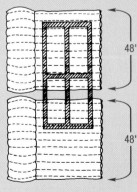

48"

48"

Two 48" widths of Warm Window = Finished shade length up to 92"/Cut shade length up to 96"

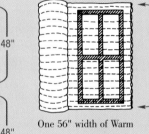

48"

48"

48"

Three 48" widths of Warm Window = Finished shade length up to 140"/Cut shade length up to 144"

56"

One 56" width of Warm Window = Finished shade length up to 52"/Cut shade length up to 56"

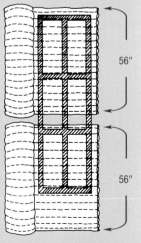

56"

56"

Two 56" widths of Warm Window = Finished shade length up to 108"/ Cut shade length up to 112"

How Many Warm Window Widths Do You Need?

To determine how much Warm Window fabric your shade will require, divide the cut shade length into 48" or 56". This is the number of Warm Window widths needed. Multiply the number of widths needed by your finished shade width to get the total number of yards required of Warm Window fabric.

21

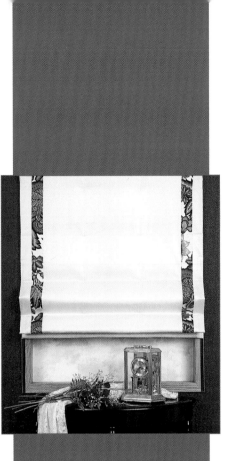

The addition of a simple border can transform a flat roman shade into an expression of decorative creativity!

1. Cut 2 (or 3) sections of Warm Window fabric a little wider than the finished width of your shade. Make sure cutting lines are perpendicular to quilted channels.

2. With the smooth-surfaced lining sides together, pin or baste sections along the top channel quilting line of stitching. To minimize waste, use the line of quilting stitches that is approximately 2" from the selvage.

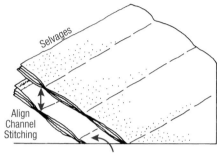

3. Machine stitch through all layers, using 10 stitches per inch. When stitching these horizontal seams, apply slight tension by holding the fabric taut behind and in front of the needle. Knot all loose threads securely.

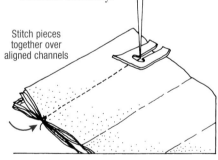

Trim the Warm Window fabric (all layers) to ¼".

4. Trim the Warm Window fabric to the required cut width as determined on the worksheet (page 20). Use a triangle to align one long side of the Warm Window fabric so it is at a right angle to the channel quilting lines. Trim as needed to square off one side, then measure and mark the desired cut width, keeping in mind that the quilting lines will run horizontally across the piece.

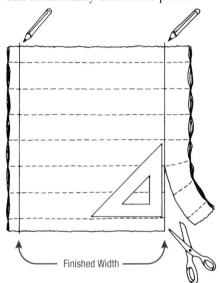

5. To trim the fabric to the required length, position the selvage edge at the bottom of the shade. Measure from the first quilted line up and mark a line perpendicular to the side edge of the shade and parallel to quilting lines. Cut along the line through all layers of the Warm Window fabric.

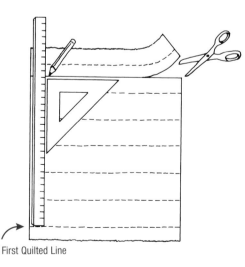

CUTTING THE COVER FABRIC

If your printed cover fabric is wide enough for your window and doesn't require seaming, take care to cut the panels for each window in the room so the print motifs line up around the room. For example, if the required cut length is 57" and the pattern repeat in your fabric is 12", you will need to cut each panel 60" long (5 pattern repeats). After cutting identical panels, cut away the excess from the same end of each one so the print is positioned the same in each panel.

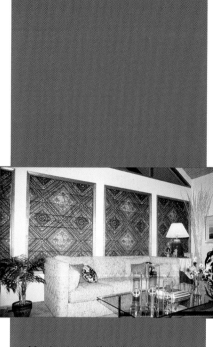

Match print motif window to window.

1. Square one edge of the cover fabric by drawing a line that is at a right angle to the selvages. Cut along the marked line.

2. Working from the squared edge, measure, mark, and cut the required length as determined on the worksheet on page 20. Make sure your fabric pattern is centered and straight on the fabric panel.

3. Working from the selvage edge, measure, mark, and cut the required width as determined on the worksheet on page 20. Be sure the cutting line is parallel to the selvage edge.

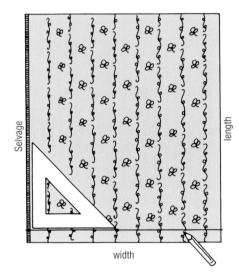

PIECING THE COVER FABRIC

More than one width of fabric may be needed to make up your finished shade. If possible, it looks best to center one full width of fabric, then split a second length of the fabric and add a piece to each side. If you are using a printed fabric for the cover, you will want to cut the panels carefully to match the print design (pattern repeat) when seaming widths together.

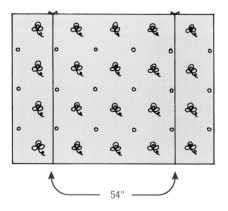

54"

To "seam" fabric panels together with Steam-a-Seam 2:

1. Place the panels right sides together and fold back the top layer at the edge until the pattern matches exactly. Adjust as needed and press the fold lightly. Turn the folded edge back onto the bottom panel, right sides together without disturbing the pattern match.

2. Place a strip of Steam-A-Seam 2 along each outer edge of the center section on the right side of the fabric.

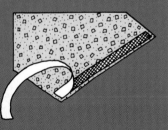

3. Fuse the panels together following Steam-A-Seam 2 directions on page 11.

4. Open out the fused panels and press flat.

5. Trim the cover fabric to the required width.

For unpatterned fabrics:

1. Cut the center section the required length.

2. Cut an additional length of fabric and cut it in half lengthwise.

3. Sew each half to a side of the center panel, using ½" wide seam allowances or follow the "No-Sew Tip" on this page. Open out the seamed sections and press flat.

4. Trim the cover fabric panel to the required width as described above.

For printed fabrics:

1. Cut 2 (or more as required) shade lengths from the printed cover fabric, being careful to cut them along the same point in the print so they will match when seamed together.

2. With the cut widths right sides together, turn back the top layer along the edge and adjust as needed so the pattern matches exactly. Press the fold lightly.

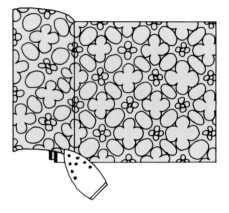

3. Being careful not to disturb the pattern alignment, fold the top layer back onto the bottom layer and pin carefully. Stitch along the pressed line. If you prefer, follow the "No-Sew Tip" on this page instead of stitching the layers together.

CONSTRUCTING THE SHADE

1. Place the right side of the cover fabric and the smooth exterior lining side of the Warm Window fabric together with the side and top edges matching. There should be 8½" of cover fabric extending below the bottom edge of the Warm Window fabric. The cover fabric will not lie flat because it was cut 3½" wider than the Warm Window fabric.

2. Pin the two fabrics together along the side edges only. Stitch together, using ¾" wide seam allowances. Zigzag stitch as close to the cut edges as possible, catching all layers in the stitching.

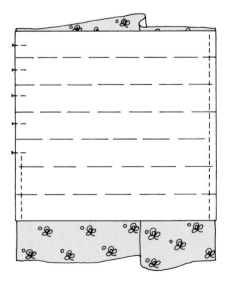

ATTACHING MAGNETIC STRIPS

Place one 3½" long magnetic strip between each row of channel quilting in the seam allowance on the wrong side of the cover fabric. There should be approximately ½" of space between each magnetic strip. To keep the magnetic polarity consistent, position the strips so the embossed arrows are pointing in the same direction. Peel off the paper backing and press firmly in place. The strips will be covered when the shade is right-side out.

- Magnetic tape strips are not required in the upper 4" of the cover fabric – this is the mounting allowance. In the finished Flat Roman shade, the depth of the top pleat may vary slightly, depending on where the upper channel line falls.

- Do not place a piece of magnetic tape on the wrong side of the cover fabric seam allowance in the lowest 4" of the shade (Warm Window fabric). Instead, position it (as shown by the dashed lines in the illustration) on the right side of the cover fabric in the seam allowance, just below the bottom edge of the Warm Window fabric. Reverse the polarity of this piece of tape as it will be turned up inside the hem.

- When the shade is turned right side out and the hem is turned up, only one layer of cover fabric will be between the magnetic tape inside the shade and the tape adhered to the wall or window frame.

Smooth Side of Insulated Fabric

Wrong Side of Designer Fabric

5. Turn the shade right side out and proceed with hemming the shade.

Turn the shade right side out and verify that the width of your shade is correct and the cover is not too loose or too tight. The cover fabric should lie smooth and flat on the front of the shade without wrinkles. Now that you've verified the width turn the shade wrong side out again.

If the cover fabric is too loose, turn the shade wrong side out and stitch slightly deeper seams than the original ones.

Sags

If the cover fabric is too tight, the side edges will curl toward the right side of the shade when placed on a flat surface. If they do, turn the shade inside out and take narrower seams to release enough cover fabric at each side to eliminate the curling. Remove the original stitching.

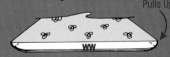

Pulls Up

HEMMING THE SHADE

Choose the correct hemming option for your shade, depending on the window style.

Option 1: Windows With No Sill

With this hem, the weight bar will be inserted in a casing made 4" up from the bottom edge of the shade. Two rows of stitching are required to form the casing. If you want the shade to seal at the bottom edge, add a strip of magnetic tape inside the shade at the bottom edge of the Warm Window and adhere a corresponding magnetic strip on the wall or trim.

1. To reduce bulk, trim all but the outer lining layer from the selvage section at the shade bottom edge. The remaining layer will be folded into the hem.

2. Place a strip of magnetic tape along the exterior lining side of the Warm Window fabric at the bottom edge just above the selvage.

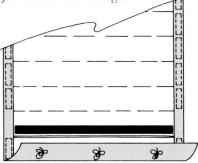

3. Fold the cover fabric up 4" and press. Fold the hem up again even with the first row of channel stitching (4" from bottom of shade).

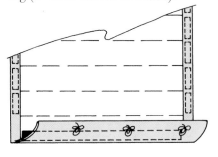

4. Stitch close to fold, using 12 to 14 stitches per inch. Use a walking foot if available for your machine. Stitch again 1" below the first row of stitching.

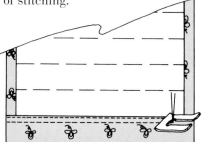

Option 2: Windows With a Protruding Sill

If your window sill protrudes, the weight bar will rest on it when the shade is lowered. To achieve a complete seal and prevent the weight bar from hitting the sill with force, wrap additional layers of Warm Window fabric around the bar when the hem is complete.

Machine stitch the hem or for a completely invisible hem, choose the hand stitching option or use Steam-A-Seam 2 for a No-Sew option.

For a machine- or hand-stitched hem:

1. Turn up and press a 4" wide hem in the cover fabric.

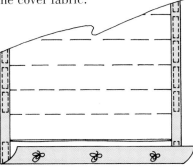

2. Turn the hem up again even with the first row of channel stitching (4" from the bottom edge of the shade).

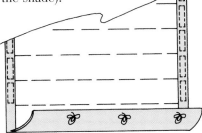

3. Machine stitch close to the fold, using 12 to 14 stitches per inch. Use a walking foot if available for your machine. If you prefer, slipstitch the hem by hand, catching all layers.

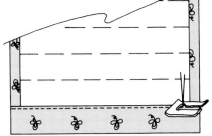

4. After installing the shade, slip the weight bar between the Warm Window layers at the bottom of the shade and hand stitch the ends closed.

No-Sew Hem

1. Trim the cover fabric hem allowance to extend only 1" below the Warm Window selvage.

2. Turn up and press a 1" wide hem in the cover fabric.

3. Position a strip of Steam-A-Seam 2 under the pressed edge and fuse following the basic Steam-A-Seam 2 directions on page 11.

4. Turn the hem up along the lowest channel quilting line and press.

5. Position a strip of Steam-A-Seam 2 under the top edge of the hem and fuse in place.

ADDING THE RINGS

To attach rings with the T-shooter, simply insert the needle of the T-shooter through all layers of fabric from the back of the shade and squeeze the trigger. This secures the rings to the shade with a transparent plastic "T" on the front of the shade.

If you prefer, you can attach the rings through the Warm Window fabric only so the plastic T's do not show on the right side of the side. If you choose this option, you must adhere the cover fabric to the lining with a light, even application of a repositionable spray adhesive. After spraying, turn the shade face up and smooth the cover fabric so it lies flat and wrinkle free. Because the lower row of rings holds the weight of the shade, reinforce with hand or machine stitching.

Choose ⅜" diameter brass or plastic rings or substitute T-rings to be applied with a T-Shooter. These will be positioned on every other channel quilting line to guide the draw cords up the shade to the screw eyes.

1. Place the shade on a large flat surface with the lining side up. Beginning at the bottom quilting line at the top edge of the hem, mark the ring positions 8" to 12" apart across the shade with the outer rings positioned no more than 2" from the side edges of the shade. Use a straight edge to mark the locations with a pencil dot. Mark additional ring positions up the shade in line with each of the bottom row ring positions, making a mark at every other channel quilting line. Pin through all layers at each ring location to hold them together and prevent shifting while you attach the rings.

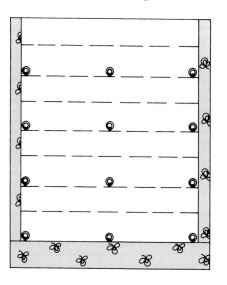

2. To attach the rings, adjust the sewing machine for bar tacking by dropping or covering the feed dogs and setting the stitch length at 0. Set the stitch width for a 4mm wide zigzag stitch. Attach the button sewing foot or open-toed embroidery foot if available. If you have a zigzag stitch on your machine, adjust the needle to a left position. (If a zigzag stitch is not possible, tack the rings in place by hand.)

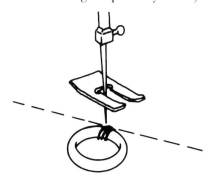

3. Place the shade and ring under the presser foot, being careful that all layers of the shade fabric are flat and smooth. Stitch through all layers of fabric, taking 8 to 10 complete stitches. To lock the stitches, change to 0 stitch width and stitch in place on the left side of the ring for several stitches. Reinforce rings in the bottom row with extra stitches since they hold the weight of the fabric and therefore must withstand the most strain.

PREPARING THE MOUNTING BOARD

In order to attach the shade to the window, you need to cut the mounting board to fit and cover it with fabric (if you wish). Here's how:

1. Cut the 1" x 2" mounting board to fit inside the window frame for inside and hybrid mounts. For an outside mount, cut it the width of the shade. You will install the board with the wider surface against the top of the window frame for an inside or hybrid mount. For an outside mount, you will install it with the wider surface against the wall.

2. Drill mounting screw holes slightly larger than the diameter of the screw. Make sure the mounting screw locations do not interfere with the location for the screw eyes (in line with the vertical rows of rings) or with the pulley location. Review the illustration of the Roman shade on page 17.

3. If you wish, cover the mounting board with a piece of muslin or a scrap of the cover fabric before attaching the screw eyes and pulley. Wrap the fabric neatly and snugly around the board and use a staple gun to secure it or use spray adhesive or Steam-A-Seam 2 to adhere the fabric to the board.

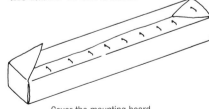

Cover the mounting board.

4. Attach screw eyes and/or pulleys to the board in line with the vertical rows of rings. Position the pulley at the operating end of the shade where you will raise and lower the shade. Use a flat screw on the inside and a screw eye on the outer end of the pulley to attach it to the mounting board. The screw eye on the outside end acts as a guide for the outermost cord. If using a plastic locking pulley, position it on the mounting board with the brass roller facing the outside edge of the shade.

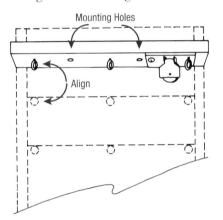

Mounting Holes

Align

When to Use a Locking Pulley

To make shade operation convenient, use a locking pulley. This type of pulley holds the shade open, thereby eliminating the need for a cleat. Use a locking pulley and a 1mm-diameter cord for shades up to 5' wide and 5' long. After attaching the pulley to the mounting board, gather all the cords neatly in order and follow the directions on page 33 for stringing the pulley.

NOTE: On larger shades, you may use standard pulleys in place of screw eyes for easier shade operation.

ATTACHING THE SHADE TO THE MOUNTING BOARD

Staple your shade to the mounting board following the directions below for the appropriate mount – inside, hybrid, or outside. If you prefer, you can attach the shade with hook and loop tape. Refer to the "Hook and Loop Option" on pages 31 & 32.

1. Measure up from the bottom of the shade and mark the finished shade length on the lining side of the shade.

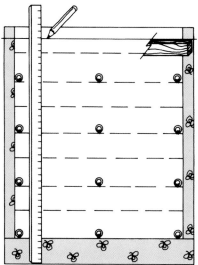

2. Measure from marked line up 2" and trim excess. Zigzag or serge all layers together.

3. Line up the top of the mounting board with the marked line and staple the shade to the board as shown, making sure that all shade layers are secured.

For an **inside mount:** Fold the shade over the mounting board and staple to the top of the board.

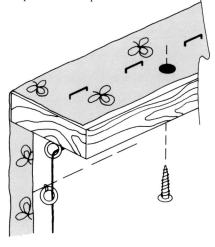

For an **outside mount:** Wrap the shade over the top of the board and staple to the back of the board.

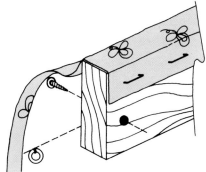

For a **hybrid mount:** Staple the right side of the shade to the narrow surface of the mounting board.

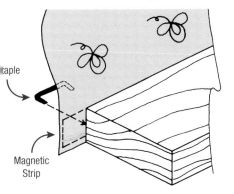

Place a strip of magnetic tape along the edge to be stapled and staple through all layers to get a straight line across the top of your shade.

Tack the shade layers together at the upper corners to prevent corners from folding over.

Hook and Loop Option

1. Choose 1", 1½" or 2" wide sew-on style hook and loop tape available at your fabric store by the yard. You will also need Steam-A-Seam 2.

2. Place the shade flat on the work table with the cover fabric against the table.

3. Measure up from the bottom of the shade to the finished shade length and trim the Warm Window layer so it is ½" longer than the finished shade length. Trim the cover fabric so it is 2" longer than finished shade length.

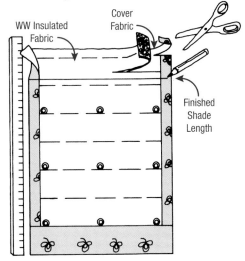

4. Fold the cover fabric down to cover the Warm Window fabric and use a strip of Steam-A-Seam 2 to fuse it in place. See the general directions for Steam-A-Seam 2 on page 11.

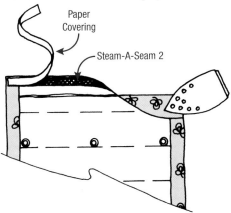

See the general directions for Steam-A-Seam 2 on page 11.

Decorator Tip

To create a contrasting hem, cut decorator fabric for shade the finished shade length plus 4½". Cut contrasting shade fabric 8½" long plus width of shade plus 3".

With cover fabric and shade bafric placed right sides together, sew ½" seam the width of your shade fabric. Lightly press seam to one side. Fold along stiched line to form hem allowance.

31

No-Sew Hook & Loop Option

1. Prepare the shade as described in steps 1-3 Hook & Loop Option.

2. At the top edge of the shade, open the Warm Window fabric to the polyethylene layer (the shiny, foil-like material) and trim away ¾" of it.

3. Place a strip of Steam-A-Seam 2 between each of the remaining layers of Warm Window fabric and fuse the layers together.

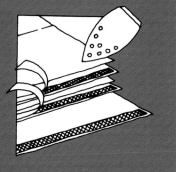

4. Use a strip of Steam-A-Seam 2 to fuse the cover fabric to the Warm Window fabric.

5. Following the manufacturer's directions, use hook-and-loop adhesive to glue the loop portion of the tape to the back of the shade.

5. Separate the hook and loop tape and cut a strip of the loop portion to match the shade width. Position it ½" below the top edge of the shade. Pin and stitch in place along each edge. Stitch in the same direction along each edge to avoid puckers in the cover fabric.

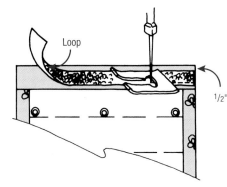
Loop
½"

6. Staple a matching strip of the hook tape to the mounting board, referring to the illustration below for the appropriate mounting method.

Inside

Outside

Loop

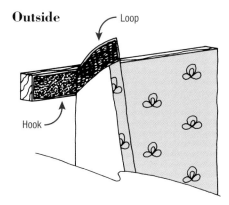

Hook

Hybrid

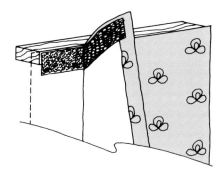

ADDING THE CORDS

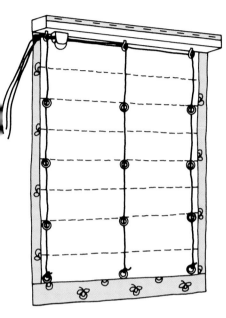

Your shade is almost ready to mount in your window. Just a few more steps and you'll be able to stand back and admire your handiwork!

1. Tie a cord to each bottom ring with a square knot. Add a few drops of white glue or clear nail polish to hold the knots securely.

2. Run each cord up through each of the rings in its vertical row and then through the screw eyes and pulley. (Refer to the directions in the sidebar for stringing the locking pulley types.)

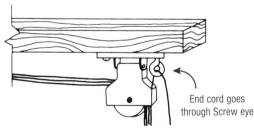

End cord goes through Screw eye

3. With even tension on all cords, tie them together a few inches below the pulley in a single knot.

4. Cut all cord ends to the same length, leaving them long enough so that you can reach them easily when the shade is completely lowered.

5. Neatly braid cords from knot to end. Tie loose ends to cord reel.

Stringing the Warm Window Cord Reel

To string the cord reel:

1. Insert the cords through the hole at the top of the cover. Hole can be enlarged with the end of a scissors or other blunt object. Slide the cover over the cords.

2. Tie the cord ends to the center rung of the "ladder" or reel base. Slide the cover down over the base of the reel, matching the notches of the ridged tabs.

3. To raise the cord reel to a higher position, slide the cover up the cord and wind the cord around the top and bottom rung of the "ladder" or base. When you reach the desired height, slide the cover over the base.

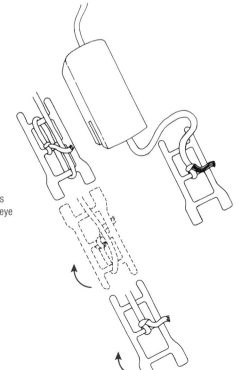

Stringing Locking Pulleys

To string a plastic locking pulley* with the recommended 1mm- or 2mm-diameter cord:

1. Remove the base bars, using a sharp tool on the side of the pulley where the bar ends show to pry them out. Slide out the brass portion of the locking mechanism.

2. String the cords over the white portion of the locking mechanism.

3. Replace the brass piece and the base bars, arranging cords evenly between prongs.

Don't put any cords between the outside prongs and pulley wall.

* For large shades with more than six cords, we recommend a standard pulley and cleat.

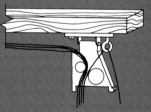

To string the metal locking pulley, use 2mm-diameter cord and guide it over the roller and along the inside of the pulley on the side with the grip holder.

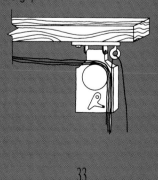

ADDING THE WEIGHT BAR

You may use the Warm Window weight bar sold as a kit or purchase ³/₈" steel and coat it with paint or varnish to prevent rust. (that could stain the finished shade)

1. If you are using the Warm Window weight bar, adjust the size to fit inside the hem, following the package directions.

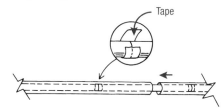
Tape

2. If you are using a steel weight bar, cut it to fit inside the hem, cutting it slightly shorter than the window width. This minimizes fabric wear at the ends caused by the bar rubbing against the window frame. File the cut ends of the bar smooth and cover them with thick tape in order to protect the cover fabric.

3. Insert the weight bar into the 1" casing at the top of the hem or at the shade bottom edge. Be sure to position the bar between lining layers to ensure a good seal. Hand stitch the ends closed over the bar ends.

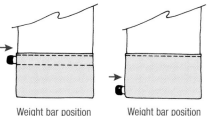

Weight bar position for hem option #1

Weight bar position for hem option #2

MOUNTING THE FINISHED SHADE

You're ready to mount your shade at the window and add the magnetic strips that seal the shade in place when it is in the lowered position. The Warm Window magnetic tape is coated with the best pressure-sensitive adhesive available. It will hold securely under most circumstances; however, some painted or textured surfaces may prevent a good bond. If the bond appears questionable, fasten each end of the strip with a small nail. If you wish, paint the tape to blend with the wall or trim. Test paint a sample to ensure good results.

1. Using long mounting screws, attach the mounting board in the correct position on the wall or inside the window. Use molly or toggle bolts if you are not able to screw into wood studs.

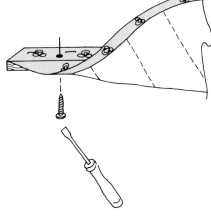

2. Mount a cleat at the operating side of the shade to secure the cords when the shade is raised. (The cleat is not necessary if you use a locking pulley.)

3. To ensure adhesion, use rubbing alcohol to clean the wall or window frame surface where the magnetic tape is to be placed.

4. Cut pieces of magnetic tape to extend the full length of each side of the window (and the length of the bottom edge if you are sealing the bottom). Place the magnetic strips against the back of the shade so that they are attracted by the magnetic strips inside the shade. If the magnetic tape strips on the inside are not attracted to the long strips on the outside of the shade so that the edges are flush with each other, you have the strip positioned with the direction of polarity reversed. Rotate the long magnetic strips 180° and replace against the shade.

5. While the tape is still magnetically attracted to the shade, place the shade against the wall or window frame. Peel the paper backing from the magnetic strip and adhere to the prepared wall or window surface, applying pressure to the magnetic tape to remove invisible air pockets between the wall and the tape. Try using a rolling pin or round can to apply concentrated pressure to the tape. A wallpaper seam roller is another option.

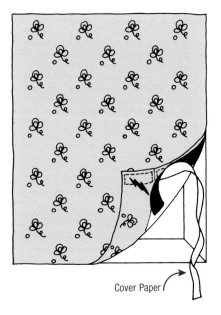

Cover Paper

6. Now take a few minutes to examine and admire your finished shade. Congratulations! You did it!

Try painting a sample of magnetic tape with your wall or trim color before adhering it to the wall to ensure good results.

USING YOUR SHADE

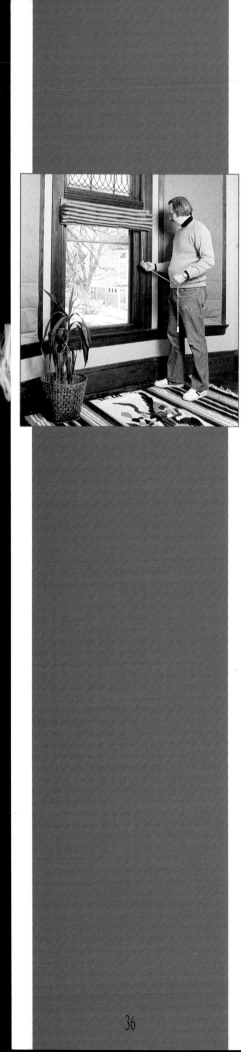

1. To raise the shade, release the magnetic seal by pulling the shade out at the bottom. Hold the bottom of the shade with a little tension while pulling the cord to raise it.

2. So that the pleats form easily and crisply each time you use it, train the shade by raising it completely, adjusting the pleats as needed, and leaving it in the fully open position for a few days. This helps the shade develop a memory so that you won't have to fuss with the pleats each time you raise the shade. You can speed up this training process before installation by loosely tying strips of fabric around the pleated shade to hold the pleats in place. Then have it steamed by your dry cleaner or leave it in a steamy bathroom with the door tightly closed for several hours. (Fill the bathtub with very hot water.)

3. Now you're ready to enjoy your energy-efficient Warm Window for years to come. You should take pride in your choice of shades of comfort, as you're feeling more comfortable in your home, saving money and conserving the earth's resources.

Please see Common Questions about Warm Window on page 80 for information about the care of your completed shade.

TOP TREATMENTS

Although your Warm Window® shade looks great alone, you might wish to add a top treatment to complement your room's decor. When considering a top treatment, keep in mind the estimated stack-up of your shade. The stack-up is the amount of room your shade will occupy when it is opened. The chart below will help determine the stack-up for your shade size. Your valance must project far enough so that the shade can be raised fully.

To Estimate The Stack Of Your Shade When Drawn Up:

If you are planning on making a valance or cornice to install over your shade, use stack width to determine the amount your valance must project from the wall. Stack depth indicates the length of your raised shade.

Length of Shade	Stack Depth	Stack Width
3 ft.	7"	4½"
4 ft.	8"	4½"
5 ft.	9"	4½"
6 ft.	10"	5"
7 ft.	11"	5"
8 ft.	12"	6"
9 ft. +	14"	6"

BALLOON ROMAN SHADE

The Balloon style lends a fuller, softer, untailored look to your Warm Window® shade. The fullness is achieved by gathering the cover fabric across the top and creating poufs at the bottom with shirring tape. This type of Warm Window shade requires about twice as much decorator cover fabric as the Flat Roman shade.

BALLOON SHADE

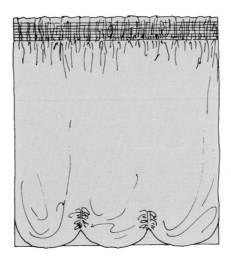

To create the balloon effect, you cut the cover fabric in five sections and sew them together. Then you sew the cover fabric to a flat panel of Warm Window fabric.

Your Balloon shade will swag more gracefully if you choose a lightweight cover fabric. Poplin, lightweight chintz, and polyester moiré are good fabric choices for Balloon shades. Balloon shades also have a deeper stack at the top than Flat Roman shades – at least $1/4$ to $1/3$ of the finished shade length will stack in the upper section of the window when the shade is fully drawn.

- Before you start your Warm Window Balloon shade project, read through Chapters 1-4.
- Follow the directions for determining your mounting option and finished shade size on page 14-15.
- For cutting and preparing the Warm Window fabric, see page 21.

MATERIALS

In addition to the Warm Window fabric, magnetic tape, decorator cover fabric and the basic tools and supplies listed in Chapter 2, you will need shirring tape. This tape contains cords which are woven into a backing. After the tape has been sewn to the cover fabric, the cords are pulled, drawing up the fabric to form gathers at the top and poufs at the bottom. Four-cord shirring tape is called for in these directions, however, if you prefer a narrower band of gathers at your shade top, two or three cord shirring tape can be substituted.
(Four-cord shirring tape can be cut down to 1, 2, or 3 cords. Zigzag or serge the cut edges to prevent fraying.) One cord shirring tape is used at the shade bottom.

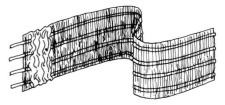

4 Cord Shirring Tape

To determine the required length of shirring tape for the top of your shade, add 2" to the cut width of the balloon panel (see page 42). You will also need a 13" length of one-cord shirring tape for each bottom pouf. See "Assembling the Balloon Shade Cover," on page 45, for directions on determining how many poufs to make in your shade.

CUTTING THE FABRICS

The cover for the Warm Window Balloon style shade is made of five sections:

• Balloon Panel – The front of the shade that faces the room.
• Side Panels (2) – Pieces that wrap to the back of the shade.
• Mounting Flap – Piece that attaches to the mounting board.
• Bottom Panel – Forms the hem.

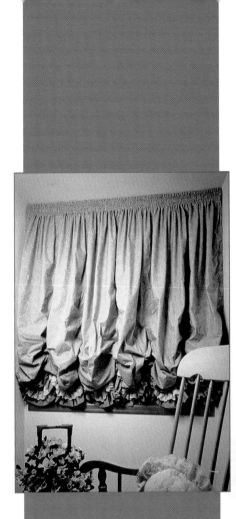

These sections are cut and assembled as shown in the directions that follow. Then they are sewn to a flat panel of Warm Window fabric.

COVER FABRIC

The cutting layout for the five sections of cover fabric depends on the size of your window and the fabric width. If the balloon panel for your shade is wider than the fabric width, you will need to seam fabric widths together as shown on page 24.

You will need the finished shade size dimension from page 12-15 to determine the cutting dimensions for the cover fabric pieces.

WARM WINDOW FABRIC

Use the Worksheet on page 20 to determine the cut dimensions for the Warm Window fabric. Cut as directed, piecing if necessary as shown on page 21-22. Set aside.

"Warm Window shades are simple to sew and easy to use in any decorating style."
Pam Lapp, Ft. Collins, CO

BALLOON PANEL

Your balloon panel is cut 1¾ times wider than the finished shade width for fullness.

Width

Finished Shade Width (from page 14-15) [ ] x 1.75 for Top Fullness

= [ ] Cut Width for Balloon Panel

Length

Finished Shade Length (from page 14-15) [ ] + ½" Allowance for Top Ruffle

+ [ ] Shirring Tape Width + ½"

(Allowance for Heading Fold Down)

+ 4" Fullness for Bottom Gathers

= [ ] Cut Length for Balloon Panel

Cut one balloon panel, using the cut length and width determined above.

SIDE PANELS

Width: 2¾"

Length

Finished Shade Length (from page 14-15) ☐ + ½" Seam Allowance

+ 4" Shirring Tape Header and Seam Allowance + 4" Fullness for Bottom Poufs

= ☐ − 3½" (Hem Allowance − ½" Seam Allowance)

= ☐ Cut Length for Each Side Panel

Cut 2 side panels each 2¾" wide and the length determined above.

NOTE: The side panels do not show on the front of the finished shade, so you can cut them across the fabric width and seam pieces together for the required length to save yardage.

MOUNTING FLAP (ELIMINATE FOR HOOK & LOOP OPTION)

Width

Finished Shade Width (from page 14-15) ☐ + 3" = ☐ Mounting Flap Width

Length: 5" Mounting Flap Length

Cut one mounting flap 5" long and the width determined above.
If you choose to mount your shade using hook and loop tape, this piece
can be omitted. See page 51 for mounting directions.

BOTTOM PANEL

Width

Finished Shade Width (from page 14-15) ☐ + 3"

= ☐ Bottom Panel Cut Width

Length: 13" Bottom Panel Cut Length

Cut one bottom panel 13" long and the cut width determined above.

NOTE: Cut this piece in the same direction as the balloon panel.

Read through the example below to review the steps in cutting your Balloon shade cover fabric.

Example #1: Balloon Panel

Width

Finished Shade Width 43" x 1.75 = 75¼" Balloon Panel Cut Width

Length

Finished Shade Length 50" + ½" + 4" Shirring Tape Width Plus ½"

+ 4" Fullness for Bottom Gathers = 58½" Balloon Panel Cut Length

Example #2: Side Panels

Width
2¾" Side Panel Cut Width

Length

Finished Shade Length 50" + ½" + 4" Shirring Tape Plus ½"

+ 4" Fullness for Bottom Gathers – 3½" Hem – Seam Allowance

= 55" Side Panel Cut Length

Example # 3: Mounting Flap

Width

Finished Shade Width = 43" + 3" = 46" Mounting Flap Cut Width

Length
5" Mounting Flap Cut Length

Example # 4: Bottom Panel

Width

Finished Shade Width = 43" + 3" = 46" Bottom Panel Cut Width

Length
13" Bottom Panel Cut Length

ASSEMBLING THE BALLOON SHADE COVER

The balloon panel is gathered across the top with shirring tape and divided into sections called poufs at the bottom. The bottom poufs correspond to vertical rows of rings on the back of the finished shade. Ease stitching at each side and the shirring tape sewn on the back of the balloon panel create the poufs at the bottom.

The poufs at the bottom are spaced 8" to 12" apart. An uneven number of poufs is more visually pleasing. There will be one more row of vertical rings on the back than the number of poufs.

To determine the number of poufs, the number of rows of rings, and the spacing between poufs for the shade you are making, use the following formulas:

- Finished width of shade divided by any number from 8 to 12 = *Number of Poufs* (should be an uneven number)
- Number of poufs + 1 = *Number of Rows of Rings*
- Balloon panel cut width − 1" (seam allowance) = _____ divided by number of poufs = *Spacing Between Poufs*

CREATING THE BOTTOM POUFS

1. With the balloon panel face down on your work surface, draw a line 14" long ¼" in from each side edge. Mark the pouf spacing determined earlier and draw a 12" long line at each pouf mark. Draw all lines up from and perpendicular to the bottom edge of the balloon panel.

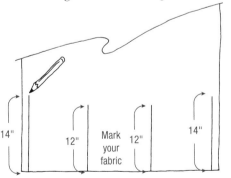

2. With the machine stitch set at basting length, stitch on the two 14" long lines only, backstitching at the top of each row of stitching to anchor. Leave long thread tails at the bottom of each row.

3. Cut a 13"-long piece of 1-cord shirring tape for each of the 12" long lines. Turn under the raw edge at the top end of each cord. Center each piece of tape over one of the marked lines. Pin in place. Stitch approximately ⅛" away from the cord on each side of it and across the top of the shirring tape to anchor the cord securely.

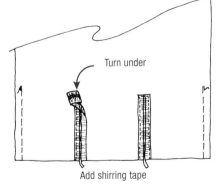

Turn under

Add shirring tape

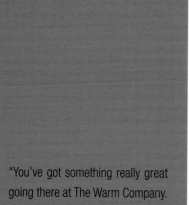

ADDING THE SIDE PANELS

1. Pin a side panel to each side edge of the balloon panel with right sides together, drawing up the basting on each side so it matches the length of the side panels. Distribute the gathers evenly so the fullness is contained within a 5" long space.

2. Stitch using a ½" wide seam allowance. Press the seams toward the side panels.

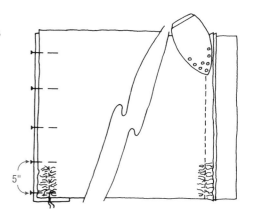

5"

SHIRRING THE TOP

1. With the wrong side of the balloon panel facing you, turn the top edge down the width of the shirring tape, plus ½".

2. Cut a piece of shirring tape the width of the balloon panel plus 2". Turn under and press 1" at each short end of the shirring tape.

3. Position the shirring tape on top of the turned edge and pin in place. Edge of tape is even with fold. Stitch ⅛" above and below each cord in the tape, backstitching at each end of the stitching to secure.

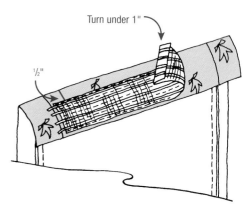

Turn under 1"

½"

ADDING THE BOTTOM PANEL
TO THE BALLOON PANEL

1. With the machine stitch length set for basting, machine stitch across the bottom edge of the balloon panel, stitching ½" from the edge.

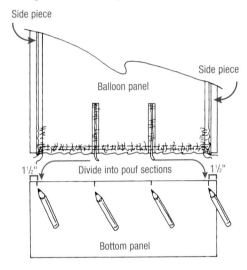

2. Subtract 1½" from each short end of the bottom panel. Divide the remaining length into the number of poufs determined on page 45, and mark.

3. Pin the balloon panel with side panels to the top edge of the bottom panel with right sides together and side edges even. Draw up the ease stitching to gather to fit and match the pouf divisions to the shirring cords on the balloon panel. Stitch ½" from the raw edges just outside the basting stitches and press the seam toward the bottom panel.

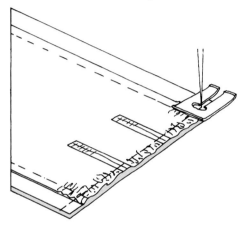

ATTACHING THE BALLOON SHADE
TO THE WARM WINDOW FABRIC

1. Place the right side of the Balloon shade (cover fabric) and the smooth exterior lining side of the Warm Window fabric together.

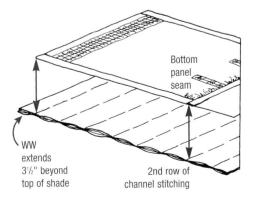

2. Align the bottom seam of the Balloon shade with the second quilted channel above the bottom edge of the Warm Window fabric and pin in place. Pin the sides together with raw edges even. The Balloon shade will not lie flat due to the extra width for turning. In addition, there should be about 4" of Warm Window extending past the top edge of the Balloon shade. You will trim this when you mount the shade.

Attach shade to WW

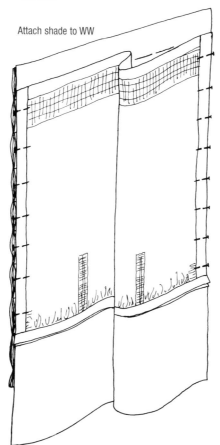

3. To check your finished shade length, measure from the bottom channel line of the Warm Window fabric just above the selvage to the top of the Balloon shade fabric. The measurement should be ½" longer than finished shade length determined earlier.

Add the mounting flap.

1. Place the mounting flap face down on the wrong side of the Balloon shade (cover fabric). With the side edges matching, lap the mounting flap into the shirred heading area 1". Pin in place at the side edges. About 3½" of the mounting flap should extend above the shirred area.

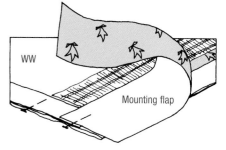

WW

Mounting flap

2. Using scant ¾" wide seam allowances, stitch the side seams from the top of the Warm Window fabric to the bottom. Stitch through all layers. Stitch again as close to the raw edges as possible, catching all layers. Use a zigzag stitch for the best results.

3. Turn the shade right side out and verify that the width is correct. The Warm Window fabric should lie flat with the cover fabric smooth across the top and bottom sections without wrinkles. Disregard the extra fullness in the balloon panel for now. If the cover fabric is too tight, the Warm Window fabric will not lie flat. Turn wrong side out and make narrower side seams, removing the first row of stitching on each side. If it is too loose, remove the excess by sewing slightly deeper side seams.

4. After turning shade wrong sides out, attach magnetic strips to the shade as directed for Roman Shade on page 25.

NOTE: If you prefer, your shade can be attached to the mounting board using hook and loop tape. If you choose this option, skip step 3. Directions for hook and loop option are on page 51.

SHIRRING THE TOP AND DRESSING THE BOTTOM POUFS

1. Pull the top shirring cords out at one end of shade and tie each one in a secure knot. Pull the cords out a little at the opposite end so that you will be able to reach them later. Pin in place to secure for now. Do not trim cords yet.

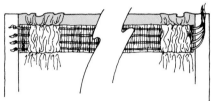

2. Turn the shade right side out and smooth out the top and bottom sections. Disregard the extra fullness in the balloon fabric for now.

3. With the Warm Window fabric facing up, smooth the side panels around the Warm Window fabric so the seams are each approximately ¾" from the edge of the Warm Window fabric. Lightly press the outer edges flat using an iron and press cloth. Stitch through all layers along each side seam line, being careful not to hit the magnetic strips inside the seam allowance with the needle.

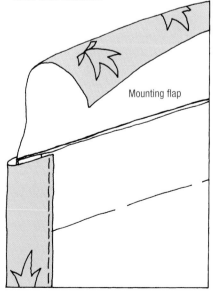

Stitch sides ¾" from shade edge

4. There should be a bit of extra fullness at each side of the shade on the front. To create a crisp edge, make a tuck at each side about ¾" deep, folding it in from the shade top edge to the top of the gathered area at the bottom of the balloon panel. Press, then pin in place. When you add the rings later, these pleats will be caught in place by the ring bar tacking.

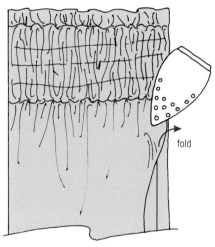

fold

5. Reach inside the top of the shade and pull the cords to gather the balloon panel to match the width of the Warm Window fabric. Distribute the gathers evenly and pull the cords up so they extend above the top edge of the ruffle. Make sure the top of the ruffle is aligned with the top of the Warm Window fabric. Warm Window fabric will extend 3½" past top of ruffle.

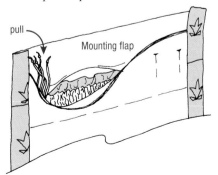

pull

Mounting flap

6. Stitch through all layers across the top of the ruffle along the first row of previous stitching (approximately ½" below the folded edge), anchoring the cords as you stitch. Trim the cords close to the stitching and dab the cut ends with white glue.

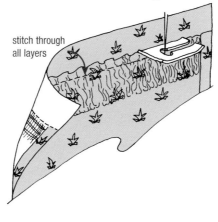

stitch through all layers

7. Reach between the balloon panel and the Warm Window fabric and pull the bottom gathering cords until the seam between bottom panel and balloon panel are even with the second channel line up from the Warm Window fabric. Knot or hand stitch the cords in place at the bottom of the shade so they won't slip while you finish the hem. Trim the cords, leaving a 1" long tail on each. Dab ends with white glue.

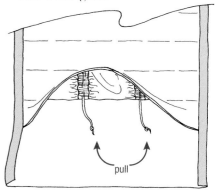

pull

FINISHING THE SHADE

1. Refer to page 26 for hemming directions. Be careful to keep the poufs out of the way as you stitch the hem in place.

2. Arrange the gathers evenly across the front of shade and pin in place to keep fabric evenly gathered while attaching rings.

3. Attach the rings to the shade, removing the pins as you work, referring to the directions on page 28.

4. Follow directions on page 29-30 for preparing the mounting board and attaching the shade.

MOUNTING YOUR SHADE

Mount the shade as described on page 35 with the following exception – the ½" ruffle at the top of the shade should extend above the top edge of the mounting board, regardless of which mounting option you have chosen. Trim away extra layers of the Warm Window to reduce the bulk.

For all mounts – line up the top edge of the mounting board with the seam of the mounting flap.

For inside mounts – the ruffle will extend above the mounting board past the opening of the window.

Inside Mount

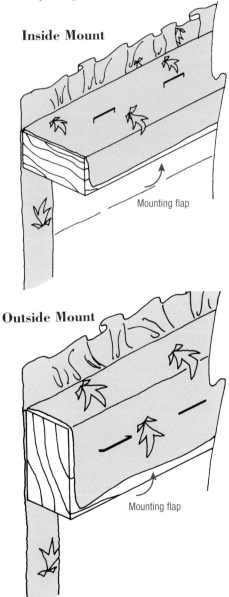

Mounting flap

Outside Mount

Mounting flap

Hybrid Mount

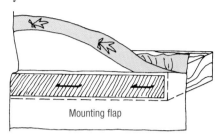

Mounting flap

Hook and Loop Mounting Option

1. Trim Warm Window fabric so it is even with the balloon shade top. Serge or zigzag the top edge of the Warm Window fabric to finish and prevent fraying.

2. Pin loop portion of hook and loop tape ½" below top edge of shade. Stitch along both long edges. Backstitch at ends.

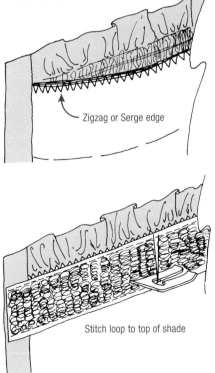

Zigzag or Serge edge

Stitch loop to top of shade

Loop portion of hook and loop tape can be applied using an adhesive made specifically for this purpose. You can find it at your local fabric store. Follow the manufacturers directions. BEFORE APPLYING LOOP, follow steps 1 & 2 on this page.

Stitch through all layers of the shade along top row of previous stitching in shirring tape.

Position loop tape to the Warm Window fabric ½" below top of shade ruffle. Hook portion of tape should be stapled to mounting board.

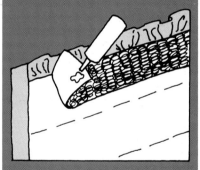

HOBBLED ROMAN SHADE

Unlike the Flat Roman shade, which is flat when lowered and pleated when open, the Hobbled shade maintains its soft folds even when the shade is lowered. The folds add interest and depth to the shade, making the style especially attractive for plain or subtly textured fabrics.

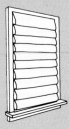

MAKING A WARM WINDOW®
HOBBLED ROMAN SHADE

To achieve the hobbled look, the outer fabric is first attached to a separate lining that wraps around the Warm Window fabric which hangs flat when lowered. When raised, the pleats create a deeper stack-up than the Flat Roman shade. You will need to purchase approximately twice as much cover fabric as you would for a Flat Roman shade.

- Read Chapters 1-4 before you start your Hobbled shade project.
- Decide which mounting option (page 14-15) you will use.
- Follow the directions on page 12-13 to determine the finished shade size.

CUTTING THE FABRICS

In addition to the Warm Window fabric, magnetic tape, decorator cover fabric and the basic tools and supplies listed in Chapter Two, you will need lining fabric for the Hobbled shade. Cut the pieces for each shade from each fabric as directed on page 55.

WARM WINDOW INSULATED FABRIC

Use the Worksheet on page 20 to determine the cut dimensions for the Warm Window fabric. Cut as directed, piecing if necessary as shown on page 21-22. Set aside.

LINING FABRIC

The lining is the base for the Hobbled shade cover fabric. You may use drapery lining or other tightly woven, medium-weight fabric. Make sure the magnetic strips and tape attract securely through the lining fabric before you buy it. The lining will be visible from the side of the finished shade so choose a color that coordinates with your cover fabric – white, beige, or a solid color.

Cut the shade lining 3½" wider and 4" longer than your finished shade length.

Lining Fabric Cut Size

Width

Finished Shade Width	" + 3½" =	Lining Cut Width

Length

Finished Shade Length	" + 4" =	Lining Cut Length

COVER FABRIC

To create the hobbled folds of your shade, the cover fabric is cut twice as long as the Warm Window fabric with an additional 4" added for the hem. Each 4" wide section of the Warm Window fabric requires an 8" length of cover fabric. Refer to the chart below when determining and cutting the cover fabric length.

To determine the cover fabric cut width, add 3¼" to the finished shade width. This allows for a double ½" wide side hem and ⅛" extension of the cover fabric beyond the Warm Window fabric.

NOTE: Before beginning refer to the general directions on page 23-24 for preparing the cover fabric.

Cover Fabric Cut Size

Width

Finished Shade Width	+ 3¼" =	Cover Fabric Cut Width

Length

Warm Window Cut Length	x 2 =	+ 4" Hem Allowance

=	Cover Fabric Cut Length

CONSTRUCTING THE HOBBLED SHADE

You can use Steam-A-Seam 2 to hem the panels instead.

1. Turn under and press a ³⁄₄" wide hem.

2. Tuck a ¹⁄₂" wide strip of Steam-A-Seam 2 between the hem layers and fuse.

3. Attach a second strip of Steam-A-Seam 2 to the first hem. Turn the hem under a second time and fuse.

1. Place the cover fabric wrong side up on the work surface. Turn up and press a 1¹⁄₂" wide hem at each side edge. Turn the raw edge in to meet the crease and press. Stitch close to the inner folded edge on each side.

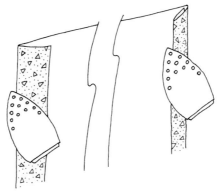

2. On the right side of the cover fabric, draw a line 12" above and parallel to the bottom edge. Divide the remaining length into 8" wide spaces, drawing lines parallel to the bottom edge of the shade and perpendicular to the sides. A pencil may be used to draw the lines since you will be stitching over them and they will be covered by the hobbles when shade is completed. Place a pin on each line at the outer edges to help with placement when pinning the lining to the cover fabric.

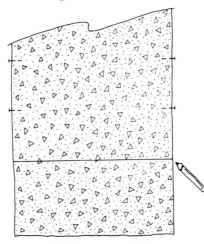

Mark lines on cover fabric

3. On the right side of the lining fabric, draw a line 4" above and parallel to the bottom edge. Divide the remaining length into 4" wide spaces, drawing lines parallel to the bottom edge of the lining and perpendicular to the sides.

4. With both fabrics right side up, center the cover fabric on the lining fabric with 1³⁄₈" of lining extending beyond the cover fabric on each side. Carefully align the marked lines on the cover fabric with the marked lines on the lining fabric and pin in place along each line.

5. Stitch the cover fabric to the lining, stitching over each marked line on the cover fabric. Begin and end the stitching ¹⁄₄" from the edges of the cover fabric. Use a walking foot if available, to help prevent the fabric layers from shifting.

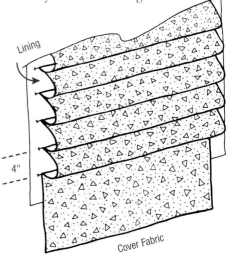

Lining

4"

Cover Fabric

6. After stitching the layers together, hold up the shade. The decorator fabric should hang in even-width folds that overlap each other by approximately 2".

ATTACHING THE HOBBLED SHADE TO THE WARM WINDOW FABRIC

1. Place the right side of your cover fabric and the smooth exterior lining side of your Warm Window fabric together. Match the top, bottom, and side edges of the lining to the Warm Window fabric, noting that the lining and cover fabric combination will not lie flat because it is 3½" wider than the Warm Window fabric. Match the stitched lines on your cover fabric with each quilted channel line on the Warm Window fabric, beginning with the second channel up from the bottom edge. Pin the sides in place.

2. Stitch a scant ¾" from the raw edges. Zigzag stitch as close as possible to the raw edges, catching all layers. Straight stitch if a zigzag machine is not available.

3. Turn your shade right side out and verify that the size is correct. If not, refer to page 25 in the directions for the Flat Roman shade to adjust the shade as needed.

4. Complete and mount your shade as directed for the Flat Roman shade, beginning on page 25.

Making No-Sew Hobbles

Cover fabric and lining can be joined using Steam-A-Seam 2. After lines are drawn, place a row of Steam-A-Seam 2 below each line marked on the lining. Pin layers together and fuse row by row.

NOTE: When measuring and marking your finished shade length, the last hobble at the top of the shade may need to be adjusted so it will fall evenly within the space below it. Adjust and zigzag or serge through all layers of the shade prior to mounting.

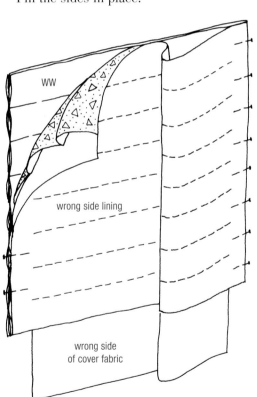

WW

wrong side lining

wrong side
of cover fabric

SIDE-DRAW SHADE

The Warm Window® Side-draw shade is perfectly suited to sliding glass patio doors, French doors, and large windows where overhead stacking area is not available. Unlike Roman style shades, the Side-draw shade is constructed with the 4" wide quilted Warm Window channels running vertically instead of horizontally. When the shade is drawn, it folds neatly into 4" wide pleats, much like a standard draw drapery.

The Side-draw features a track with a magnetized face that makes it possible to magnetically seal the shade at the top as well as at the sides. The track is available as a kit; see page 62 for the components you will need to purchase separately.

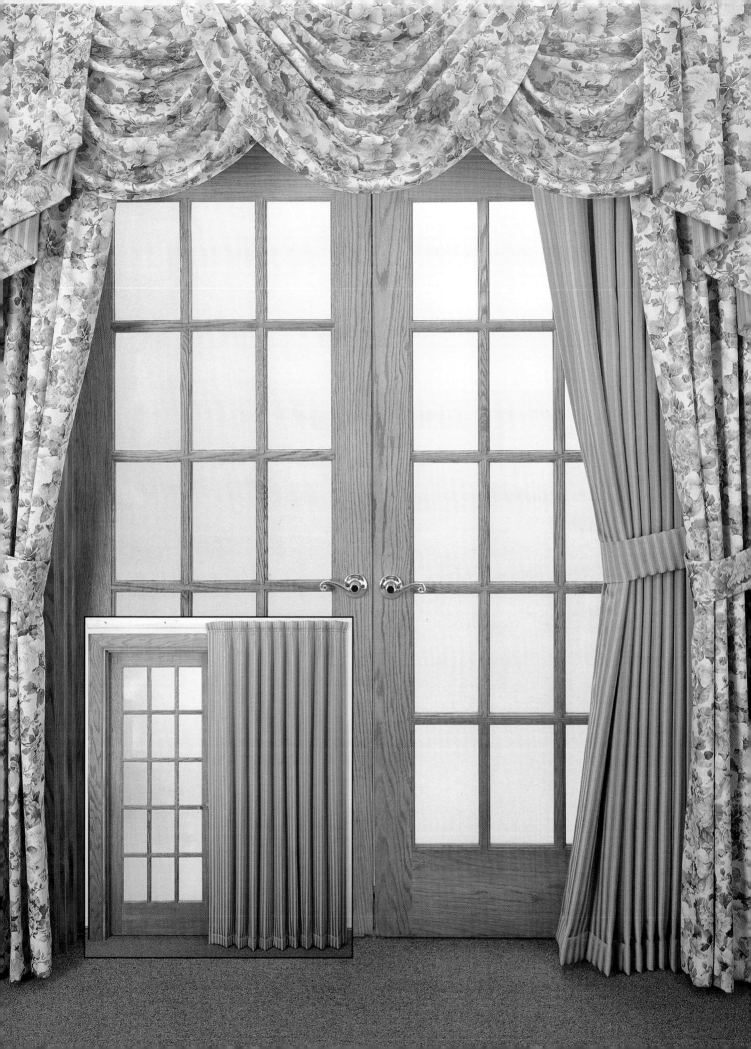

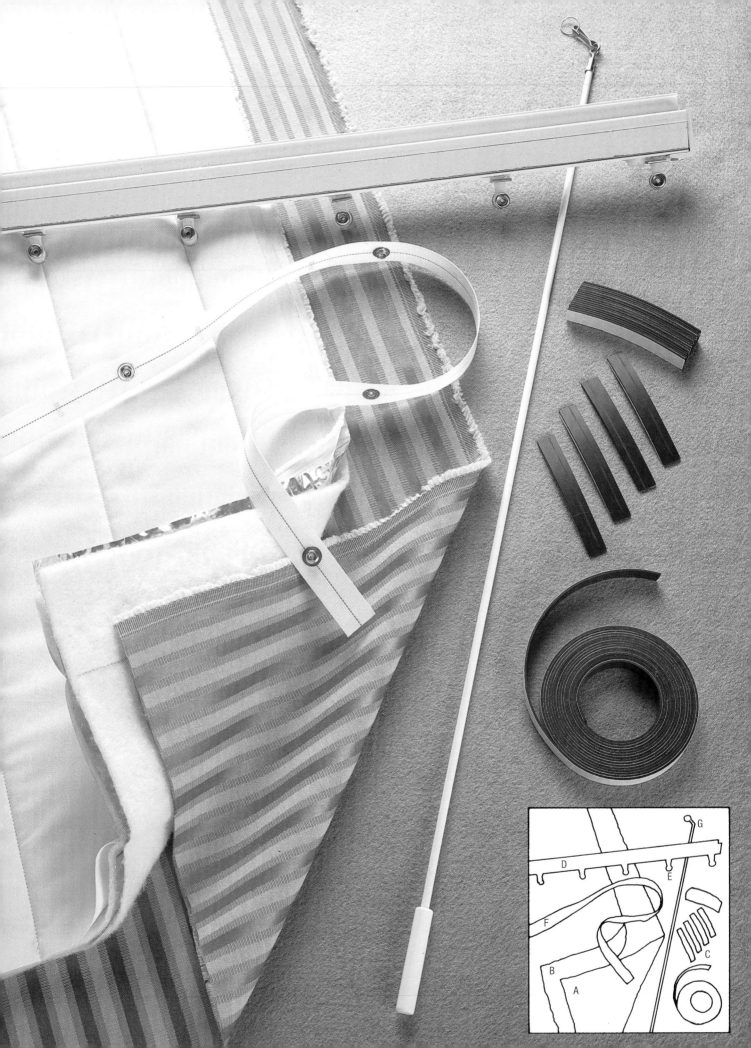

ANATOMY OF A SIDE-DRAW SHADE

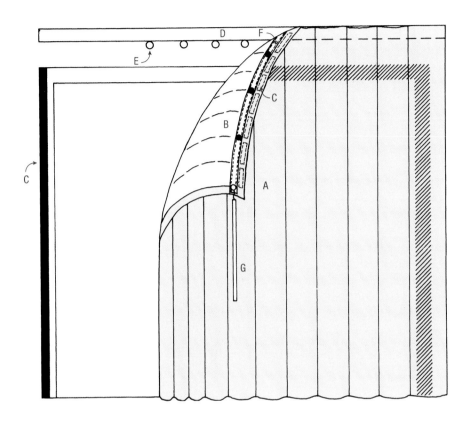

A. **Cover Fabric:** The side of your shade that faces the room will be covered with the decorator fabric of your choice.

B. **Warm Window Fabric:** Quilted channels run vertically on the Side-draw shade.

C. **Magnetic Tape:** Self-adhesive magnetic tape at the top and sides of the shade attract to corresponding magnetic tape along the sides of the window or door and the magnetized face of the track.

D. **Track:** The Side-draw Track Kit includes a 103½" length of track, ample length for a standard sliding glass patio door or French doors.

The kit also includes:

E. **Sliders:** A series of 14 easy-rolling, heavy-duty carriers hold the shade securely in place, flush with the face of the track.

F. **Snap Tape:** Snaps are spaced 8" apart on this ⅞" wide nylon "sew-on" tape. Each track kit comes with 112" length of tape with 14 attached snaps.

G. **Drapery Wand:** The 30" long wand has a metal clip with a ring that hooks onto a carrier for easy operation of the shade.

MAKING WARM WINDOW®
SIDE-DRAW SHADES

MATERIALS FOR THE SIDE-DRAW SHADE

Refer to chapters 1–3 for general information about Warm Window and shade components before beginning your Side-draw project.

Warm Window Fabric

Before you purchase your fabric, be sure to determine how many fabric widths you will need to cover your window and how long the widths must be. Follow the directions on the worksheet on page 68. Measure and cut the Warm Window fabric the size of the finished shade plus allowance for shrinkage. Remember quilted channels run vertically on the Side-draw shade.

Decorator Cover Fabric

The side of your shade that faces the room will be covered with the decorator fabric of your choice. Choose a tightly woven, light to medium weight cotton or cotton polyester blend fabric. Make sure that the magnetic tape and strips will attract through the fabric before purchasing it.

Warm Window Edge Seal

The Side-draw shade requires self-adhesive magnetic tape at the top and sides to attract to corresponding magnetic tape along the sides of the window or door and the magnetized face of the track. Convenient, pre-cut $3\frac{1}{2}$" long strips are positioned inside the shade at the top of each vertical channel; continuous tape is placed inside the shade at the sides. Refer to the Side-draw shade worksheet in the Appendix to determine quantities of each for your project.

Please read the information on pages 10-11 about tools and materials and workroom tips before you begin your Side-draw project.

Warm Window Side-draw Track Kit

The Side-draw Track Kit includes a $103\frac{1}{2}$" length of track that can be cut to size with a hacksaw. If your window or door is wider than $103\frac{1}{2}$", track sections can be installed end to end to equal the required length. The track is designed for use with an outside mount. Remove the flange at the top of the track to adapt it for an inside mount.

The kit includes all of the components needed to make and install your Side-draw shade, except for fabric and magnetic strips.

CHOOSE A MOUNTING OPTION

Outside Mount

The Side-draw track is designed for simple installation with the most effective results when used as an outside mount. The track is positioned above the door or window with screws drilled through the flange to secure it to the wall.

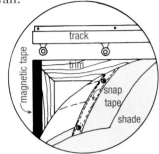

If your door or window is surrounded by decorative trim, your shade can be made to seal magnetically by placing magnetic strips on the outer edges of the trim (see photo, page 64).

If you prefer, your door or window glass can be fully exposed when your shade is open. If this is the case, add to the shade width so it will stack off the glass area when not in use. A 1" x 2" wood mounting board is added at the stationary side of the shade to hold the magnetic tape and provide a flush surface for the shade to seal.

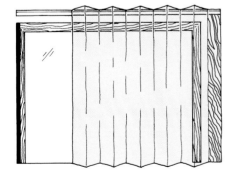

If your door or window has no trim, the magnetic tape can be placed directly on the wall in line with the ends of the track. Or if preferred, 1" x 2" mounting boards can be installed vertically to hold the magnetic tape and provide a flush surface for the shade to seal.

Inside Mount

To adapt the Side-draw track for an inside mount, the flange at the top of the track is removed. See page 74. The track is screwed to the inside top of the window or door opening so it is flush with the wall or trim surrounding the glass.

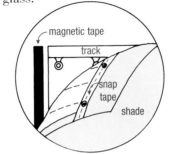

To achieve a magnetic seal for your inside mount shade, choose one of two options.

1. Make the shade the exact width of the door opening and add ½" trim to the inside of the opening for magnetic tape placement.

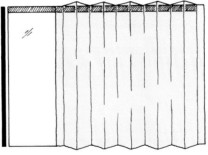

Option 2: Inside mount

2. Make the shade at least 1½" wider than the door opening and place the magnetic tape on the wall near the edge of the opening.

See page 64-67 for complete measuring instructions.

Your Side-draw shade can be designed to open to the right or the left, depending on your door position and style preference. One side will be stationary.

Or, you may choose to make two Side-draw panels that open from the center out. In this case, both outside edges will be stationary.

MEASURING FOR AN OUTSIDE MOUNT

When measuring for your Side-draw shade, consider which direction your shade will open and whether there are any obstacles that might impede the shade operation. Distance to an adjacent wall, fireplace, light switch, or heat vent can be critical.

To determine how much space your shade will occupy when it is open, refer to the "Stacking Allowance Chart" on page 76.

Determine the width of the shade for an outside mount by deciding how far outside the casing you want the shade to be and measure accordingly. If you are considering an outside mount, choose one of the following options:

1. Shade extends to the outer edges of the trim, covering trim completely when closed. Magnetic tape is placed on the outer edges of the trim.

2. Shade stacks beyond door opening, exposing all of the window glass when opened. A mounting board is added to the stationary side of the shade for attaching the magnetic tape.

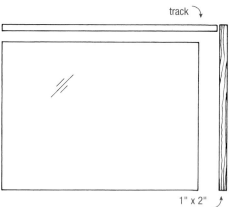

TO DETERMINE FINISHED SHADE WIDTH AND LENGTH FOR AN OUTSIDE MOUNT

Width

Measure the width of the door opening including the trim and desired width beyond.

If your door has no trim, add at least ¾" to each side of finished shade width for magnetic tape placement.

To this width, add extra to allow for slight shrinkage during construction. For shades up to 60" wide add 1" to the finished shade width. For shades from 60" to 108" add 1½" to the finished shade width.

Width Measurement (from above)

+ 1½" minimum for option 1.

+ ___ Shrinkage Allowance (1" or 1½"; see above)

= ___ Finished Shade Width

Length

You can mount the track at the desired height above the window or door trim when using an outside mount. The top of the track must be at least 3½" above the trim for the sliders to move freely. The track must also be located at least ½" below the ceiling line. Mark the desired track position on the wall and measure from where top of track will be to the floor.

___ Distance from Top of Trim to Floor

To this measurement add at least 3½" for track and sliders.

= ___ Finished Shade Length

The use of a top treatment can add a finished look to your Side-draw project. Check the stacking allowance chart on page 76 for shade projection before planning your top treatment.

MEASURING FOR AN INSIDE MOUNT

Using a steel measuring tape for accuracy, measure across the window or door casing from one inside edge to the other. To make sure the opening is square, measure diagonally from corner to corner in both directions. Both measurements should be the same. If not, choose the outside mount and turn to page 64.

Be sure to measure at the top, bottom, and center of the window or door and use the largest of the three measurements.

If you are considering an inside mount, choose one of the following options:

1. Shade fits completely inside door opening. Trim must be added inside door opening for placement of magnetic tape.

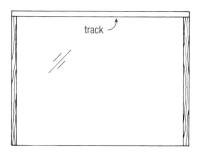

2. Shade extends beyond door opening at sides at least ¾" on each side. Magnetic tape is placed on wall or trim.

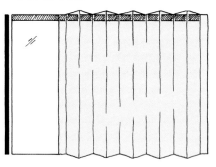

TO DETERMINE FINISHED SHADE WIDTH AND LENGTH FOR AN INSIDE MOUNT

Width

Measure exact width of door or window opening.

☐ Exact Width of Opening

Add at least ¾" to each side if shade will extend past opening.
(Option 1 page 66)

To this width, add extra to allow for slight shrinkage during construction.
For shades up to 60" wide, add 1" to the finished shade width.
For shades from 60" to 108", add 1½" to the finished shade width.

☐ Width of Opening Measurement
(from step 1 above)

+ ☐ Shrinkage Allowance

+ 1½" minimum for Option 1

= ☐ Finished Shade Width

Length

Measure from the inside top of the window or door opening to the floor.

☐ Exact Length of Opening

NOTE: You will install the track in the door opening at the top,
and need at least a 1" wide space for the track to fit.
If not, choose the outside mount and go to page 64.

☐ Length of Opening Measurement

− ½" ☐ Subtract ½" so shade will
not touch the floor.

= ☐ Finished Shade Length

When choosing a fabric for your Side-draw shade, consider its durability and stain repellency.

SIDE-DRAW SHADE WORKSHEET

Using the shade dimensions determined for the desired mounting method, determine the cut sizes for the cover fabric and the Warm Window fabric for your shade.

Warm Window Cut Width = Finished Shade Width

Warm Window Cut Length = Finished Shade Length

To determine Warm Window yardage, divide finished shade width by 48" or 56". Round up to the nearest whole number. Multiply finished shade length by the required number of widths to get total yards.

Cover Fabric Cut Width

Shade Width

+ 3" Seam Allowance

= Side-draw Cover Fabric Cut Width

Cover Fabric Cut Length

Shade Length

+ 10" (3" for top hem and 6" for bottom hem plus a 1" allowance for shrinkage which may be trimmed when top is finished.)

= Side-draw Cover Fabric Cut Length

Cover Fabric Yardage

To determine how many fabric widths required for your shade:

Shade cut width divided by cover fabric width =
Number of fabric widths required.

÷ =

To determine required yardage:
Number of fabric widths required x cover fabric cut length =
Required yards of cover fabric.

x =

CUTTING THE WARM WINDOW INSULATED FABRIC

Now that you've measured your windows, determined the finished and cut fabric sizes and purchased your fabrics, you are ready to cut and assemble your Side-draw shade.

Most Side-draw shades are wider than one width of the Warm Window fabric, making it necessary to piece one or more widths together. Follow the directions for piecing as shown on page 22 for Flat Roman shades, aligning the two outermost quilting channels and stitching along the stitching line. Trim seams close to stitching. Remember the quilted channels run vertically on your Side-draw shade.

1. Cut the required number of lengths of Warm Window fabric, making sure that the cut edges are straight and perpendicular to the Warm Window channels. Use a carpenter's square or triangle to mark the cutting lines.

2. Sew the lengths together as needed. Trim and press. (See page 22.)

3. At the side edge of the Warm Window fabric where the shade will remain stationary, draw a cutting line 1½" from the first row of channel quilting stitches. Cut on the line.

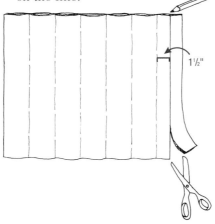

4. Measure the desired cut width from the cut edge to the opposite side of the Warm Window fabric and draw the second cutting line. Make sure it is parallel to the quilted channel lines and perpendicular to the top and bottom cut edges. Cut.

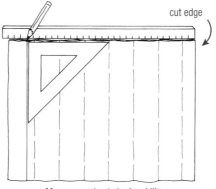

Measure and cut shade width

Most Side-draw shades are wider than one width of the Warm Window fabric, making it necessary to piece one or more widths together.

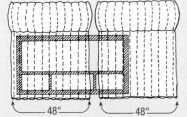

2 widths 48" WW = Finished shade width up to 96"

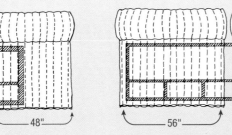

2 widths 56" WW = Finished shade width up to 112"

CUTTING THE COVER FABRIC

Piecing Fabric Widths

If you need more than one fabric width for your shade, center one full width on the window, adding panels of equal width to the side edges. This is true for both patterned and unpatterned fabrics. Refer to page 23-24 for piecing and pattern matching directions. You may use the No-Sew option with Steam-A-Seam 2 if you prefer.

If you are making two Side-draw shades that open from the center out, thay can be sealed together when closed using magnetic tape.

Position tape as directed in step 4, this page, on one panel. Place tape on the other panel in the seam allowance on the Warm Window fabric side. Make sure tape attracts before positioning.

1. Square one cut end of the cover fabric by drawing a line perpendicular to the selvages. Use a straight edge or carpenter's square. Cut along the marked line.

2. To cut the fabric into the required number of widths, measure from the squared end using the cut length of the cover fabric from page 68. If using a print, make sure the fabric pattern is centered and straight on the piece. Cut the required number of widths, making sure that the pattern repeat will match all the way across the shade.

3. If your shade requires more than one width, join the cover fabric lengths, matching the pattern as shown on page 23-24. See the note about piecing fabric widths, on page 23-24.

4. Cut the prepared panel to the required cover fabric cut width, making sure that the cutting lines are perpendicular to the squared top and bottom edges.

CONSTRUCTING THE SIDE-DRAW SHADE

1. Position the Warm Window fabric and the cover fabric with right sides together and the side edges even. The cover fabric should extend 6" below and 4" above the top of the Warm Window fabric. Stitch each side seam, using a ¾" wide seam. Stitch again close to the raw edges, using a zigzag stitch if available.

2. Turn the shade right side out. The cover fabric should lie flat and smooth across face of shade. If the fabric is too loose, restitch seams in a little farther. If cover fabric is too tight, remove stitching and stitch a smaller side seam.

3. Turn shade wrong side out.

4. Cut 2 pieces of magnetic tape the length of the shade minus 6". Peel away the paper backing and position the tape along the outer edges of the shade on the cover fabric side within the seam allowance. The end of each strip should be 3" from the top of the shade.

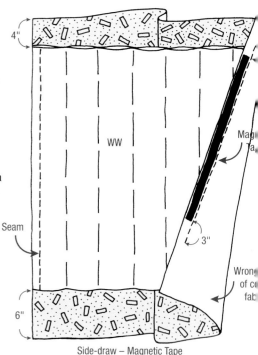

Side-draw – Magnetic Tape

5. At the bottom of the cover fabric, turn up a 3" wide hem and press. Turn again and press to make a doubled 3" wide hem. Pin in place.

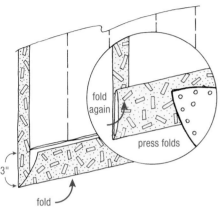

6. Position the shade with the cover fabric face up. Insert the spray adhesive can between the cover fabric and the Warm Window fabric and apply a very light and even mist of adhesive on the fuzzy surface of the Warm Window fabric. Smooth the cover fabric in place, eliminating any wrinkles and press lightly using a warm iron and a press cloth.

HEMMING THE BOTTOM

1. Remove the pins holding the hem in place. For weight, place two magnetic strips in each channel along the width of the shade parallel to the bottom. Strips may need to be cut shorter to fit into end sections. Drapery weights, available at most fabric stores, may be substituted for the magnetic strips. These can be stapled through the Warm Window or applied with a glue stick. Three 1" wide weights per channel will be required.

2. Re-pin the hem allowance in place and hand or machine stitch close to fold through all layers.

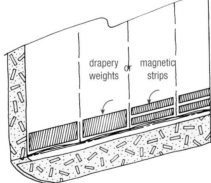

NOTE: The shade must be flat when applying spray adhesive. If your table isn't large enough, place the shade on the floor. If spray adhesive is not used, see page 74 for tacking cover fabric with Quicker Quilter.

To make a No-Sew Hem, fuse the bottom hem in place using 2 strips of Seam-A-Seam 2 placed side by side just under the top folded edge of the hem. Fuse following the general directions for Steam-A-Seam 2 on page 11.

HEMMING THE TOP

Use a clear "see through" quilters ruler to make marking placement lines fast and accurate.

With smooth lining side of the Warm Window facing you, mark placement lines for magnetic strips and snap tape.

For an outside mount

1. Draw a line 2" below and parallel to the top edge of the shade. Draw a second line 1" below the first line.

2. Place 2 rows of magnetic strips above the first marked line 2" from top of Warm Window, placing a strip between each vertical channel. Make sure that the polarity of the magnets is the same by positioning all the arrows in the same direction.

3. Fold shade cover fabric over top edge of Warm Window, concealing magnetic strips. Edge of cover fabric should line up with remaining marked line 3" from top of shade. If necessary, trim cover fabric even with the marked line.

4. Fuse the cover fabric hem in place with Steam-A-Seam 2 or machine baste close to the edge.

For an inside mount

1. Draw the first line 1½" from the top edge of the shade. Draw the second line 1" below the first line.

2. Place two rows of magnetic strips above the first marked line 1½" from top of Warm Window, placing a strip between each vertical channel. Make sure that the polarity of the magnets is the same by positioning so all arrows point the same direction.

3. Fold shade cover fabric over top edge of Warm Window, concealing magnetic strips. Edge of cover fabric should line up with remaining marked line, (2½" from top of shade.) If necessary, trim cover fabric even with marked line.

4. Fuse the cover fabric hem in place with Steam-A-Seam 2 or machine baste close to the edge.

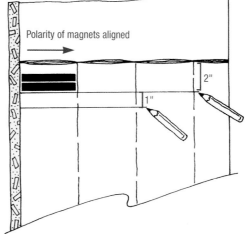

Polarity of magnets aligned

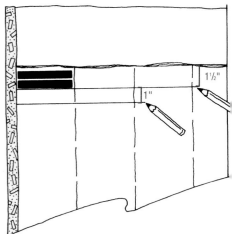

APPLYING THE SNAP TAPE

1. Cut a strip of the snap tape to match the width of the shade. Pin the tape to the back of the shade with the bottom edge 3" from the top edge of the shade for an outside mount or 2¼" from the top edge for an inside mount.

2. At the stationary edge, there should be a 1½" wide channel (page 69). The first snap is placed on the first channel line 1½" from the cut edge.

3. The next snap is positioned in line with the next channel 8" over.

4. The remaining snaps (8" apart) should line up with every other quilted channel and the last snap should be at least 1½" from the opening end of the shade. The snap tape will have to be cut to get the correct spacing.

5. Using a zipper foot, stitch close to each long edge of the snap tape, backstitching at ends. Stitch both sides in the same direction to help prevent puckers.

NOTE: If the last snap does not fall on a channel line, an additional snap must be sewn in line with the next channel over from the edge.

Clip snap tape at each channel line where there is no snap to enable shade to fold more easily.

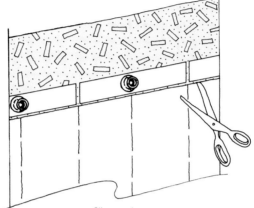

Clip snap tape

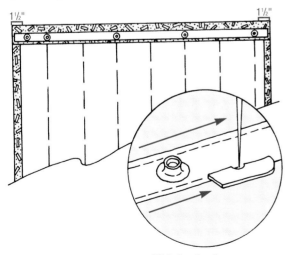

Stitch directionally

FINISHING THE SHADE

At the stationary end of the shade, you can substitute hook and loop tape for magnetic strips to keep the shade in place. Sew in place prior to installing the shade.

NOTE: Track is fitted with a blocking screw designed to keep the last carrier from moving when shade is drawn. This screw may need to be repositioned when the shade is installed. Using a slotted screwdriver, adjust the position of the blocking screw so it holds the last carrier in line with the last snap on the shade.

Because some fabrics don't bond as well as others with the spray adhesive, it is a good idea to use a Quicker Quilter (or hand tacking) to attach the cover fabric to the Warm Window fabric along the channel quilting lines wherever there is a corresponding snap at the top. Place tacks about 12" apart along each line.

Fold the shade along the quilt lines as it will fold when hung in the open position. Tie with wide strips of fabric and steam press. Leave folded and tied to dry for at least 24 hours to set the memory of the folds.

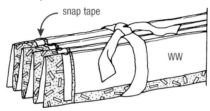
snap tape

WW

Installing the Track

For an inside mount:
1. Score the flange along the back of the track with a utility knife and snap it off.

2. Drill holes in the track directly through the groove on the bottom. One hole at each end and two additional holes evenly spaced along the track are sufficient.

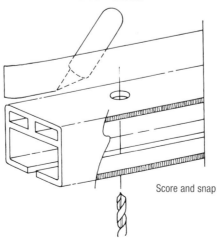
Score and snap off flange

For an outside mount:
1. Drill holes through the flange at the top of the track, referring to inside mount step 2 for the hole spacing.

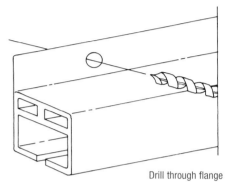
Drill through flange

Installing Your Shade

1. To install your completed shade, simply snap it to the carriers in the track, beginning with the last snap at the stationary end.

2. Before attaching the snap at the opening end of the shade, hook the ring at the end of the drapery wand over the first carrier. Then snap shade in place.

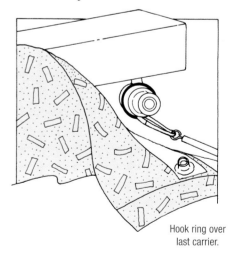
Hook ring over last carrier.

Installing Magnetic Tape

1. See page 35 for installing the magnetic tape on the wall or trim at the ends of the shade.

2. At the stationary end of the shade, the addition of a small finishing nail at top and bottom of the shade through all layers will keep the shade from releasing when pulled closed.

Add A Tieback

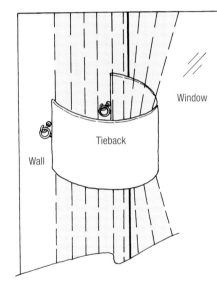

To keep your shade neatly held back when open, the addition of a tieback is recommended. Use a scrap of fabric from your shade or a contrasting fabric for a decorative accent. In addition to the fabric, 4" wide buckram the length of the tieback and two cup hooks are needed.*

1. Using a cloth measuring tape, with the shade open, measure from the outside of the shade around to the inside where your hook will be placed. Pull measuring tape as tight as you want the tieback.

2. Cut the buckram the length measured in step 1.

3. Cut cover fabric the length of the buckram plus 2" and $9\frac{1}{8}$" wide.

4. With right sides together and long edges aligned, sew cover fabric using a $\frac{1}{2}$" seam. Press seam open.

5. Turn cover fabric right side out. Slip buckram inside tube and position seam on center back.

6. Fold ends in and press. Stitch ends close to fold.

7. Sew a plastic ring at the center of each end.

Install a cup hook outside the shade at the desired height. Place a second hook inside the shade even with the outside hook. Hook tieback over outside hook and loop around to inside hook when shade is open. Unhook tieback from either end when closing shade.

One hook is placed on the wall or trim outside the shade and a second hook is placed behind the shade at the same level.

To add flair to tieback, add a border of piping or braid and a tassle or two.

SIDE DRAW STACK CHART

If you are planning on making a valance or cornice to install over your shade, use stack width to determine how far your valance must project from the wall to allow room for the shade to open. Stack depth indicates the width of your shade when it is fully opened.

Width of Shade	Stack Depth	Stack Width
3 ft.	7"	4½"
4 ft.	8"	4½"
5 ft.	9"	4½"
6 ft.	10"	5"
7 ft.	11"	5"
8 ft.	12"	6"
9 ft. +	14"	6"

If you wish to have your shade clear the window glass when open, add the stack depth to the finished shade width for stacking allowance.

APPENDIX

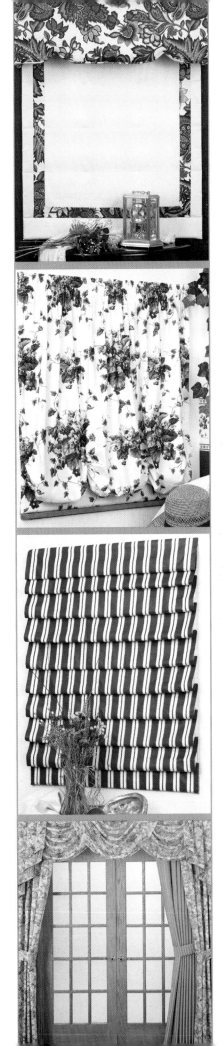

GLOSSARY OF HELPFUL TERMS

Clearance: The distance a shade projects out from the wall.

Cornice: Fabric and batting are wrapped around a board that surrounds the window top on three sides. A "soft cornice" may be fabricated using batting and two layers of fabric. Bottom edge may be straight or scalloped, or any shape desired.

Cut Length/Width: The length or width the fabric is cut with all hem and seam allowances added.

Finished Length/Width: The length or width the shade is to be when it is finished and installed.

Grain: The relationship between the crosswise and lengthwise threads of a woven fabric. In woven fabric, the crosswise threads run perpendicular to the lengthwise threads. If the threads are not perpendicular to each other, the fabric is off grain and the seams will not hang straight, but will pull to one side or the other. In addition, the pattern repeat may be off and difficult to match. Carefully examine the decorator fabric of your choice to check the grainline and do not buy off-grain fabric for your shades.

Header: A narrow edge above a line of gathers that forms a ruffle.

Hobble: In decorating, loose folds of fabric that are "hobbled" or held in position permanently. (They look like the pleats in a Roman shade, even when the shade is lowered.)

Hybrid Mount: Combines features of inside and outside mounts. Mounting board fits inside window opening and shade overlaps opening on each side.

Inside Mount: Shade and mounting board fit inside window opening.

Outside Mount: Shade and mounting board install outside window frame.

Pattern Repeat: The distance between the beginning and end of a printed pattern. Most often, the vertical repeat is the most important consideration in shade making because you need to match pattern repeats. To determine the size of the vertical repeat, measure lengthwise from the same spot on one motif within the repeat to the same spot in the next identical motif. This will help you in determining the required yardage for your shade to ensure enough for matching.

Pouf: The gathered section of fabric at the bottom of the balloon shade.

Press Cloth: A protective layer of fabric placed under iron to prevent scorching. Cotton or cotton blends are best.

Right Side: This is the printed or finished side of the fabric. If your fabric has little difference between right and wrong sides, mark the right side with a piece of tape.

RST: Abbreviation for right sides together.

Scallop: See pouf.

Seam Allowance: The distance from the outside edge of the fabric to the stitching line.

Selvage: The lengthwise edge of the fabric that is finished to prevent raveling. Check your cover fabric to see if the selvage is very tight. If it is, trim it away so the fabric will lie flat. The selvage of Warm Window fabric is about 2½" wide. Use it at the bottom hem of your shade.

Shirring Tape: A strip of woven fabric with cords running lengthwise. When you pull the cords, they evenly gather the tape and the fabric to which it has been stitched. Shirring tape is available in widths of 1" to 5".

Stack: The amount of space occupied when a drapery or shade is fully opened. Roman shades have an overhead stack and drapery-style shades have a vertical stack.

Stacking Allowance: The amount added to the width or length of the shade so it will clear the window glass when opened.

Swag: A length of fabric stretched between two outside brackets or swag holders. A traditional swag can be made and mounted on a board with separate side pieces or jabots.

Valance: A section of fabric mounted on a rod or board. Can be gathered, ruffled, poufed or pleated for fullness. Lower edge of fabric hangs free.

COMMON QUESTIONS
ABOUT WARM WINDOW

Can I paint or wallpaper over the magnetic tape?

You can successfully paint the magnetic tape before it is installed with most paints. Try your paint on a small sample first to insure that it is compatible. You can also wallpaper over the magnetic tape if the paper has a smooth surface. Flocked paper or grasscloth may prevent a strong seal.

Do I have to use magnetic tape?

Using the magnetic tape is the best way to seal the shade around the window. The shade will still reduce heat loss without the magnetic seal, but not nearly as much – just like your refrigerator would not do a very good job with the door left partly open. If you are tempted to make a shade without the edge seal, consider putting magnetic strips inside the shade anyway as they will stiffen the edge of the shade which will then fold more neatly as it is raised.

How should I cover a sliding glass door?

The Side-draw system was designed for use on a sliding glass door, however, the flat Roman style can be used as successfully. Consider making one Roman shade using an outside mount so the shade will gather entirely above the door when raised or two separate shades can be made. The addition of a vertical 1" x 4" board in the center of the door provides a place to attach the magnetic tape.

How often should the shades be raised or lowered?

Raising the shades daily is recommended. Leaving the shades open during daylight will allow solar heat gain to help warm your home on many winter days.

How can I reduce condensation?

The amount of condensation which will accumulate on windows is related to the amount of moisture in the air and the temperature of the window glass.

When a Warm Window shade is installed, the window glass will remain much colder since it is no longer being warmed by the escaping room heat. The colder glass would normally increase condensation except the Warm Window vapor barrier stops much of the moist air from reaching the glass. Usually the accumulated condensation will be about the same after installation of the Warm Window as it was before.

If condensation is a problem, it may be the result of excessive moisture in the air from many indoor plants, the lack of an exhaust duct and fan for showers, a clothes dryer, or from a missing vapor barrier in the crawl space under the floor. Opening the shade daily and drying up any accumulated condensation moisture will help prevent mildew. A strip of open cell foam weather-strip applied at the bottom of the glass will help to absorb moisture before it reaches the sill.

A container of desiccant such as Daisy Crystals left behind the shade will also help.

Should I use a locking pulley or a standard pulley with a cleat?

The locking pulley is convenient and eliminates the need to tie the cord to a cleat to hold up the raised shade, however if the shade is large and more than six cords are needed, a standard pulley and cleat are recommended. On very large shades, standard pulleys in lieu of screw eyes will require less effort to raise the shade.

What can I do to safely and neatly store the dangling cords when my shade is open?

The Warm Window cord reel was designed to solve the problem of dangling cords which pose a serious threat to small children and pets. The cord reel is a two part device you attach to the end of your shade cords. Excess cord is simply and conveniently wound inside until the shade is lowered.

What can I do about window hardware that interferes with the shade?

The operating crank of a casement window which prevents the shade from closing properly may be replaced with a T-handle available from your Warm Window retailer. A large sliding glass door handle can often be replaced with a smaller one available from a builders' hardware dealer.

Why is the cover fabric cut 3½" wider than the shade fabric? Does a wider shade need more than 3½"?

The 3½" slack is taken up in seam allowances and wrap around for the magnetic tape strips. No matter what the width of the shade fabric, only 3½" is needed for seam allowances and wrap around. Refer to page 20.

Can I wash my shade?

Washing in water may cause uneven shrinkage of the different materials in the system unless all of the materials are pre-washed – which is done by some Warm Window customers. However, since pre-washing removes the sizing from the cover fabric and the shade has a greater tendency to wrinkle, we don't recommend washing.

What about dry cleaning?

We recommend that you care for Warm Window shades in much the same way as you care for upholstered furniture. A spray-on and vacuum-off upholstery cleaner may be used or you may prefer an on-site upholstery cleaning service. If the shade must be dry cleaned, it should only be dry cleaned by the non-immersion method. If the shade is immersed in cleaning solvent, as in the Stoddard, perchloroethylene or Valclene methods, the adhesive on the magnetic tape will likely be dissolved. After any washing or cleaning, spray both sides with fabric protector.

How else can I reduce the heat loss in my home?

After attic insulation and Warm Window shades, the most important step is to reduce cold air infiltration by caulking. Caulk the joints outside where the siding meets the window trim. On a windy day, if you still feel cold air coming in around the window, it may be necessary to remove the trim and fill the space between the window frame and the 2 x 4 framing with tightly packed fiberglass or urethane foam from a can that does not have a fluorocarbon propellant. Also check for cold air coming in around the edge of doors and your fireplace and caulk accordingly. Cold air may be coming in around the electrical outlets on outside walls, so install inexpensive foam gaskets under the face plates, available at hardware stores.

FLAT ROMAN SHADE WORKSHEET

Warm Window:

Use for Flat Roman, Hobbled and Balloon Styles.

Finished Shade Width ☐ " (This is your Warm Window Cut Width)

Finished Shade Length ☐ " + 4" = ☐ " (Warm Window Cut Length)

Note: When measuring Warm Window Cut Length, do not include the selvage edge in your measurement. Although it is left on, it will be turned up inside the hem. Measure and cut Warm Window length by starting with the bottom most 4" channel.

Window (Describe) _____

Finished Shade Width ☐

Warm Window Cut Width ☐

Finished Shade Length ☐

Warm Window Cut Length ☐

Yards Required ☐

Window (Describe) _____

Finished Shade Width ☐

Warm Window Cut Width ☐

Finished Shade Length ☐

Warm Window Cut Length ☐

Yards Required ☐

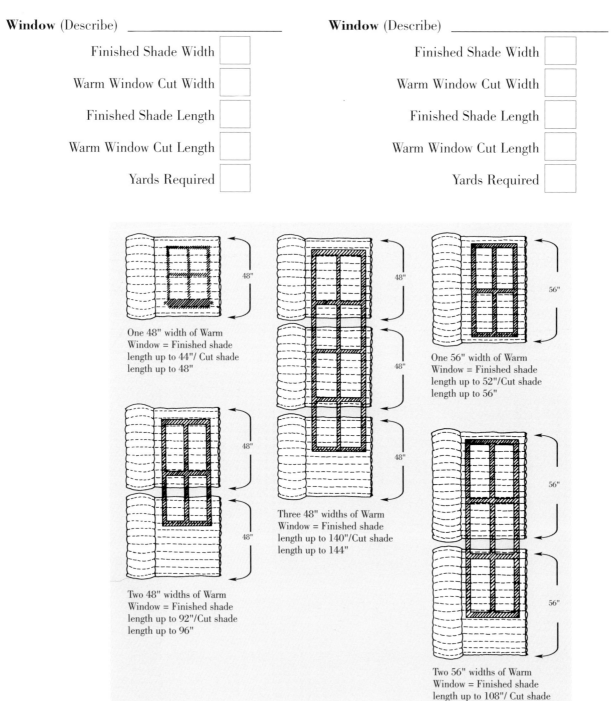

One 48" width of Warm Window = Finished shade length up to 44"/ Cut shade length up to 48"

Two 48" widths of Warm Window = Finished shade length up to 92"/Cut shade length up to 96"

Three 48" widths of Warm Window = Finished shade length up to 140"/Cut shade length up to 144"

One 56" width of Warm Window = Finished shade length up to 52"/Cut shade length up to 56"

Two 56" widths of Warm Window = Finished shade length up to 108"/ Cut shade length up to 112"

FLAT ROMAN SHADE WORKSHEET

Cover Fabric:

Finished Shade Width [ ] " + 3½" = [ ] " Cover Fabric Cut Width

Finished Shade Length [ ] " + 12½" = [ ] " Cover Fabric Cut Length

Cover Fabric Yardage Formula:

To determine how many fabric widths required for your shade:

Shade Cut Width divided by cover fabric width = Number of widths required (round up to next whole number).

[ ] ÷ [ ] = [ ]

To determine required yardage:

Number of fabric widths required x cover fabric cut length = Required yards of cover fabric.

[ ] x [ ] = [ ] " ÷ 36" = [ ] yds. (round to next ⅛ yd.).

For Shades Using More Than One Width Of Fabric:

If you fabric has a pattern, you need to calculate extra yardage required for matching pattern widths.
Use the formula below to determine adjusted cut length.

Cover fabric cut length [ ] ÷ pattern repeat [ ] = [ ] (round to nearest whole number.)

# of repeats determined above [ ] x pattern repeat [ ] = [ ] (this is your adjusted cut length.).

HOBBLED SHADE WORKSHEET

Lining Fabric:

Finished Shade Width [ ] " + 3½" = [ ] " Lining Cut Width

Finished Shade Length [ ] " + 4" = [ ] " Lining Cut Length

Cover Fabric:

Finished Shade Width [ ] " + 3¼" = [ ] " Cover Fabric Cut Width

Warm Window Cut Length [ ] " x 2 = [ ] " + 4" = [ ] Cover Fabric Cut Length

Cover Fabric Yardage:

To determine how many fabric widths required for your shade:

Shade cut width divided by cover fabric width = Number of widths required (round up to next whole number).

[ ] ÷ [ ] = [ ]

To determine required yardage:

Number of fabric widths required x cover fabric cut length = Required yards of cover fabric.

[ ] x [ ] = [ ] " ÷ 36" = [ ] yds. (round to next ⅛ yd.).

Window (Describe) _____

Finished Shade Width	[ ]
Cut Fabric Width	[ ]
Finished Shade Length	[ ]
Cut Cover Fabric Length	[ ]
Yards Required	[ ]

Window (Describe) _____

Finished Shade Width	[ ]
Cut Fabric Width	[ ]
Finished Shade Length	[ ]
Cut Cover Fabric Length	[ ]
Yards Required	[ ]

Window (Describe) _____

Finished Shade Width	[ ]
Cut Fabric Width	[ ]
Finished Shade Length	[ ]
Cut Cover Fabric Length	[ ]
Yards Required	[ ]

Window (Describe) _____

Finished Shade Width	[ ]
Cut Fabric Width	[ ]
Finished Shade Length	[ ]
Cut Cover Fabric Length	[ ]
Yards Required	[ ]

BALLOON SHADE WORKSHEET

Cover Fabric:

Balloon Panel

Finished Shade Width ☐ " x 1.75 = ☐ " Cut Width for Balloon Panel.

Finished Shade Length ☐ " + ½" for top ruffle + ☐ (Shirring tape width + ½")

+ 4 " ☐ (Fullness for bottom gathers) = ☐ " Cut Length for Balloon Panel.

Side Panels (Cut Two)

Width = 2¾"

Finished Shade Length ☐ " + ½" seam allowance + ☐ (Shirring tape width + ½")

+ 4" ☐ (Fullness for bottom gathers) = ☐ " – 3½" = ☐ Cut Length for each Side Panel.

Mounting Flap

Finished Shade Width ☐ " + 3" = ☐ " = Mounting Flap Width.

Length = 5"

Bottom Panel

Finished Shade Width ☐ " + 3" = ☐ " = Bottom Panel Cut Width.

Length = 13"

To determine cover fabric yardage required; use the space below to diagram your cutting layout.

Pieces drawn in approximate size proportion

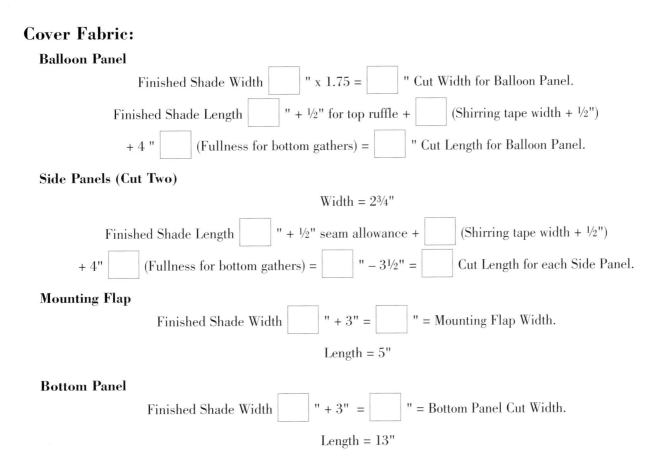

Cover Fabric Yardage:

To determine how many fabric widths required for your shade:

Shade Cut Width divided by cover fabric width = Number of widths required (round up to next whole number).

☐ ÷ ☐ = ☐

To determine required yardage:

Number of fabric widths required x cover fabric cut length = Required yards of cover fabric.

☐ x ☐ = ☐ " ÷ 36 = ☐ yds. (round to next ⅛ yd.).

SIDE-DRAW SHADE

Warm Window:

Finished Shade Width ☐ " + 1–1½" shrinkage allowance = ☐ " Warm Window Cut Width

Finished Shade Length ☐ " = Warm Window Cut Length

To determine Warm Window yardage, divide finished shade width by 48" or 56". Round up to next whole number. Multiply finished shade length by required number of widths to get total yards needed.

Window (Describe) _____

Finished Shade Width	☐
Warm Window Fabric Width	☐
Finished Shade Length	☐
Warm Window Cut Length	☐
Yards Required	☐

Window (Describe) _____

Finished Shade Width	☐
Warm Window Fabric Width	☐
Finished Shade Length	☐
Warm Window Cut Length	☐
Yards Required	☐

Window (Describe) _____

Finished Shade Width	☐
Warm Window Fabric Width	☐
Finished Shade Length	☐
Warm Window Cut Length	☐
Yards Required	☐

Window (Describe) _____

Finished Shade Width	☐
Warm Window Fabric Width	☐
Finished Shade Length	☐
Warm Window Cut Length	☐
Yards Required	☐

To determine magnetic tape quantity required:

Finished Shade Length ☐ " x 4 = ☐ " = Amount of magnetic tape required.

Finished Shade Width ☐ " ÷ 4 = ☐ x 2 = ☐ Number of 3½" magnetic strips required for top of shade.

If using magnetic strips in bottom of shade, double the above quantity.

SIDE-DRAW WORKSHEET

Cover Fabric:

Finished Shade Width ☐ " + 3" = ☐ " Cover Fabric Cut Width

Finished Shade Length ☐ " + 10" = ☐ " ☐ " Cover Fabric Cut Length

Cover Fabric Yardage Formula:

To determine how many fabric widths required for your shade:

Shade Cut Width divided by cover fabric width = Number of widths required (round up to next whole number).

☐ ÷ ☐ = ☐

To determine required yardage:

Number of fabric widths required x cover fabric cut length = Required yards of cover fabric.

☐ x ☐ = ☐ " ÷ 36" = ☐ yds. (round to next ⅛ yd.).

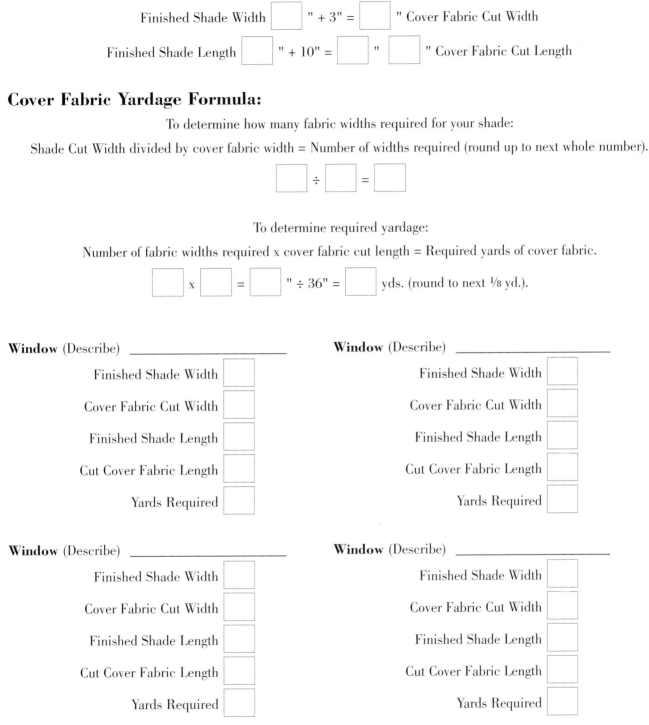

Window (Describe) _____

Finished Shade Width ☐

Cover Fabric Cut Width ☐

Finished Shade Length ☐

Cut Cover Fabric Length ☐

Yards Required ☐

Window (Describe) _____

Finished Shade Width ☐

Cover Fabric Cut Width ☐

Finished Shade Length ☐

Cut Cover Fabric Length ☐

Yards Required ☐

Window (Describe) _____

Finished Shade Width ☐

Cover Fabric Cut Width ☐

Finished Shade Length ☐

Cut Cover Fabric Length ☐

Yards Required ☐

Window (Describe) _____

Finished Shade Width ☐

Cover Fabric Cut Width ☐

Finished Shade Length ☐

Cut Cover Fabric Length ☐

Yards Required ☐

WARM WINDOW® MATERIALS CHART

For use with all Roman Shade Styles. Note: Magnetic tape (continuous) quantities are for hem option #1. For hem option #2 you will need magnetic tape equal to 2x shade length only.

Shades to 52" Long — One Width 56" Warm Window Fabric → Shades to 108" Long — Two Widths 56" Warm Window Fabric →

Shades to 44" Long — One Width 48" Warm Window Fabric → Shades to 92" Long — Two Widths 48" Warm Window Fabric → Shades to 140" Long — Three Widths 48" Warm Window Fabric

SHADE WIDTH	24"	30"	36"	42"	48"	54"	60"	66"	72"	84"	96"	108"	120"
NUMBER OF PULLEYS OR SCREW EYES	4	4	4	5	5	6	7	8	9	10	11	12	13
SHADE LENGTH up to 32"													
Yards Cord	6	6	8	10	11	13	14	16	19	23	27	31	36
Rings	12	16	20	24	24	28	28	32	36	40	44	48	52
3½" Magnetic Strips	16	16	16	16	16	16	16	16	16	16	16	16	16
Feet Continuous Magnetic Tape	9	10	11	12	13	14	15	16	17	19	21	23	25
up to 40"													
Yards Cord	7	7	9	12	12	15	15	18	21	25	30	34	39
Rings	16	16	20	24	24	28	28	32	36	40	44	48	52
3½" Magnetic Strips	20	20	20	20	20	20	20	20	20	20	20	20	20
Feet Continuous Magnetic Tape	10	11	12	13	14	15	16	17	18	20	22	24	26
up to 48"													
Yards Cord	8	8	11	13	14	17	17	20	24	28	32	37	42
Rings	20	20	25	30	30	35	35	40	45	50	55	60	65
3½" Magnetic Strips	24	24	24	24	24	24	24	24	24	24	24	24	24
Feet Continuous Magnetic Tape	11	12	13	14	15	16	17	18	19	21	23	25	27
up to 56"													
Yards Cord	9	9	12	15	15	18	19	22	25	30	35	40	46
Rings	24	24	30	36	36	42	42	48	54	60	66	72	78
3½" Magnetic Strips	28	28	28	28	28	28	28	28	28	28	28	28	28
Feet Continuous Magnetic Tape	12	13	14	15	16	17	18	19	20	22	24	26	28
up to 60"													
Yards Cord	10	10	13	16	18	20	21	24	28	33	39	43	49
Rings	28	28	35	42	42	49	49	56	63	70	77	84	91
3½" Magnetic Strips	30	30	30	30	30	30	30	30	30	30	30	30	30
Feet Continuous Magnetic Tape	13	14	15	16	17	18	19	20	21	23	25	27	29
up to 63"													
Yards Cord	11	11	14	18	18	22	22	26	30	35	41	46	52
Rings	28	28	35	42	42	49	49	56	63	70	77	84	91
3½" Magnetic Strips	34	34	34	34	34	34	34	34	34	34	34	34	34
Feet Continuous Magnetic Tape	14	15	16	17	18	19	20	21	22	24	26	28	30
up to 76"													
Yards Cord	12	12	16	19	20	24	24	28	32	38	43	49	56
Rings	32	32	40	48	48	56	56	64	72	80	88	96	104
3½" Magnetic Strips	38	38	38	38	38	38	38	38	38	38	38	38	38
Feet Continuous Magnetic Tape	15	16	17	18	19	20	21	22	23	25	27	29	31
up to 84"													
Yards Cord	13	13	17	21	21	25	26	30	35	40	46	52	59
Rings	36	36	45	54	54	63	63	72	81	90	99	108	117
3½" Magnetic Strips	42	42	42	42	42	42	42	42	42	42	42	42	42
Feet Continuous Magnetic Tape	16	17	18	19	20	21	22	23	24	26	28	30	32
up to 96"													
Yards Cord	15	15	19	24	24½	29	29	34	39	45	52	58	65
Rings	40	40	50	60	60	70	70	80	90	100	110	120	130
3½" Magnetic Strips	48	48	48	48	48	48	48	48	48	48	48	48	48
Feet Continuous Magnetic Tape	18	19	20	21	22	23	24	25	26	28	30	32	34
up to 108"													
Yards Cord	17	17	22	27	30	32	33	38	44	50	57	64	72
Rings	48	48	60	72	72	84	84	96	108	120	132	144	156
3½" Magnetic Strips	54	54	54	54	54	54	54	54	54	54	54	54	54
Feet Continuous Magnetic Tape	20	21	22	23	24	25	26	27	28	30	32	34	36
up to 124"													
Yards Cord	19	19	24	30	30	36	36	42	48	55	63	70	78
Rings	52	52	65	78	78	91	91	104	117	130	143	156	169
3½" Magnetic Strips	62	62	62	62	62	62	62	62	62	62	62	62	62
Feet Continuous Magnetic Tape	22	23	24	25	26	27	28	29	30	32	34	36	38